Beyond Words

Amanda Kennedy-Christina

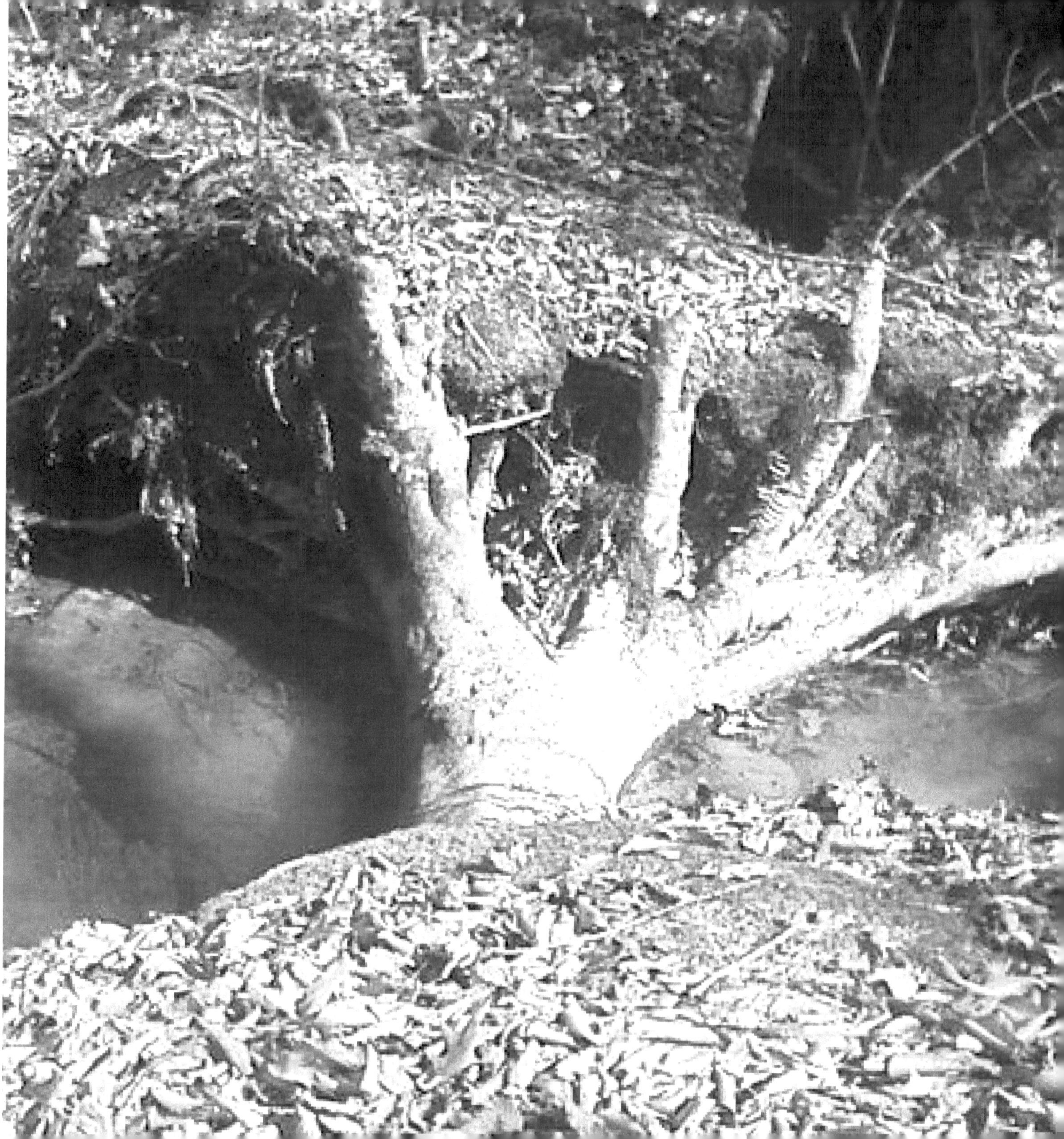

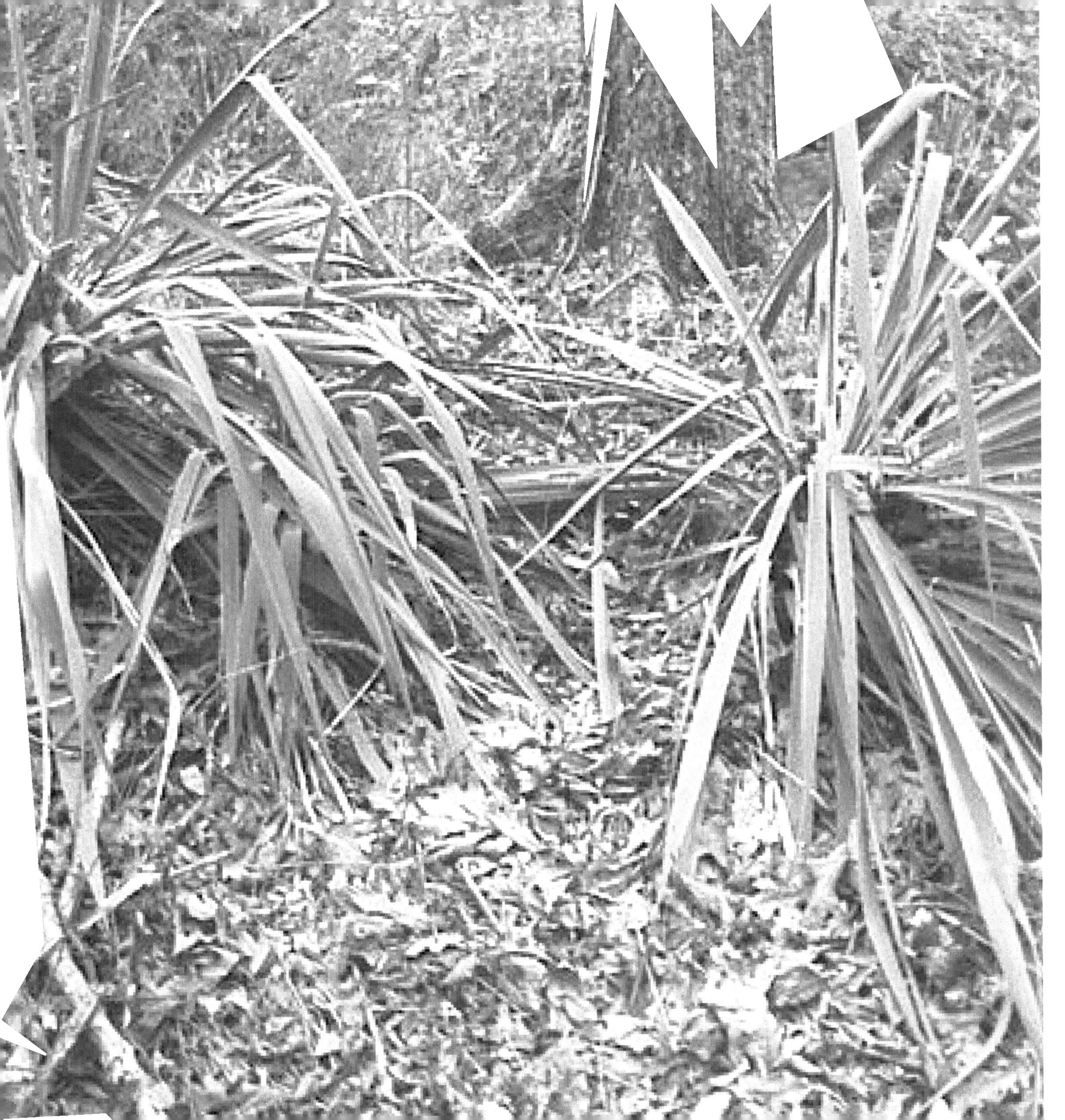

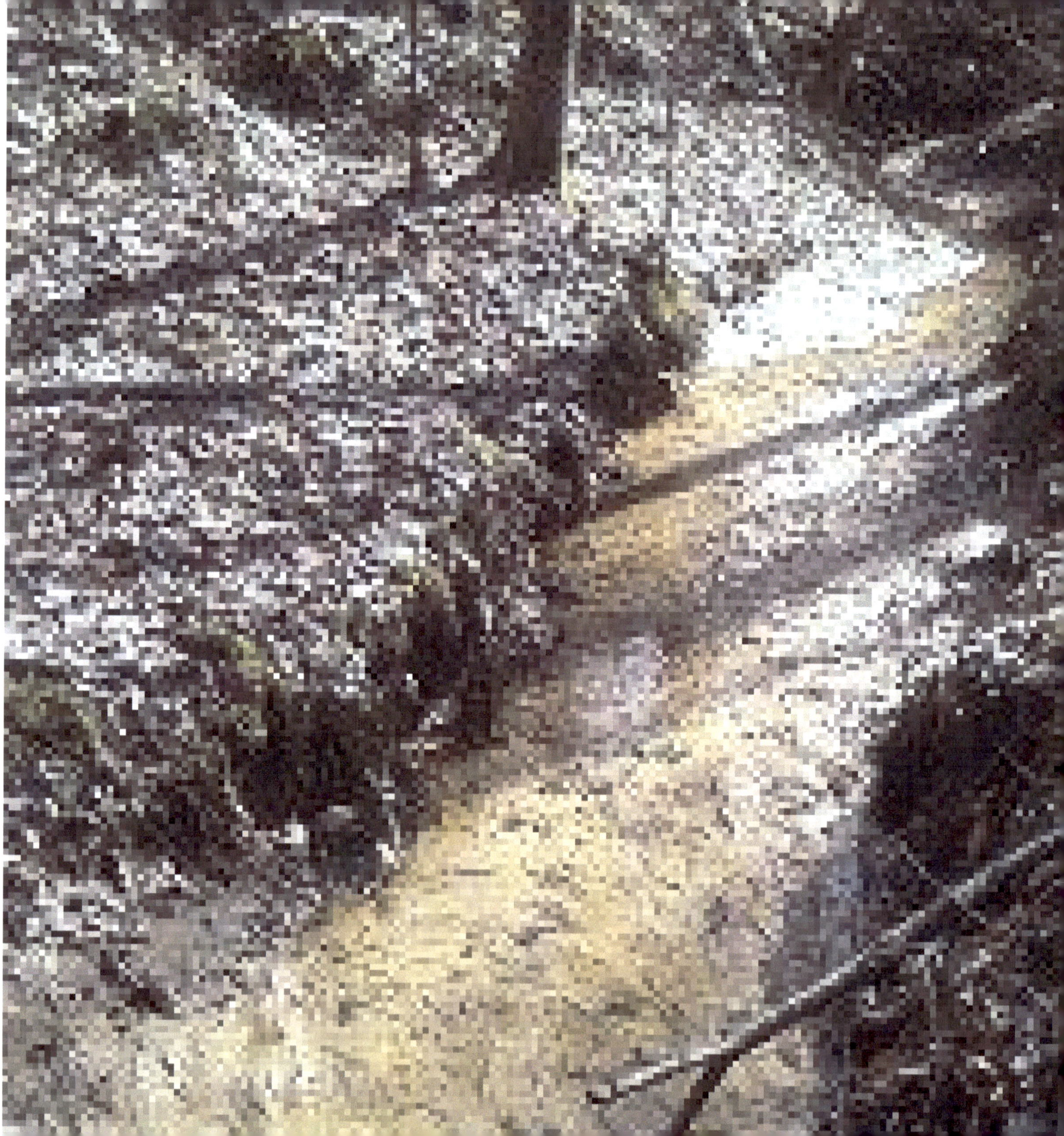

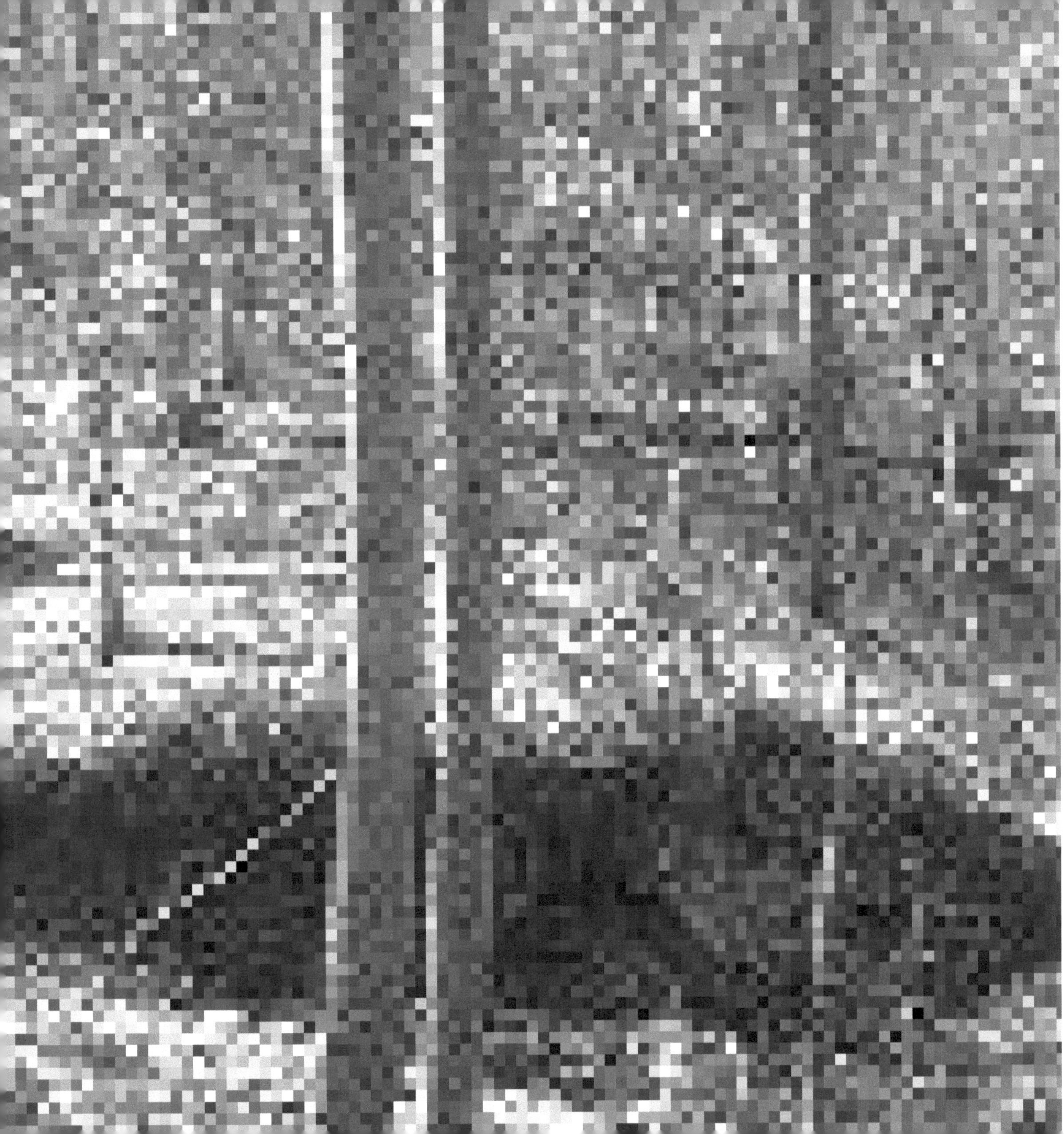

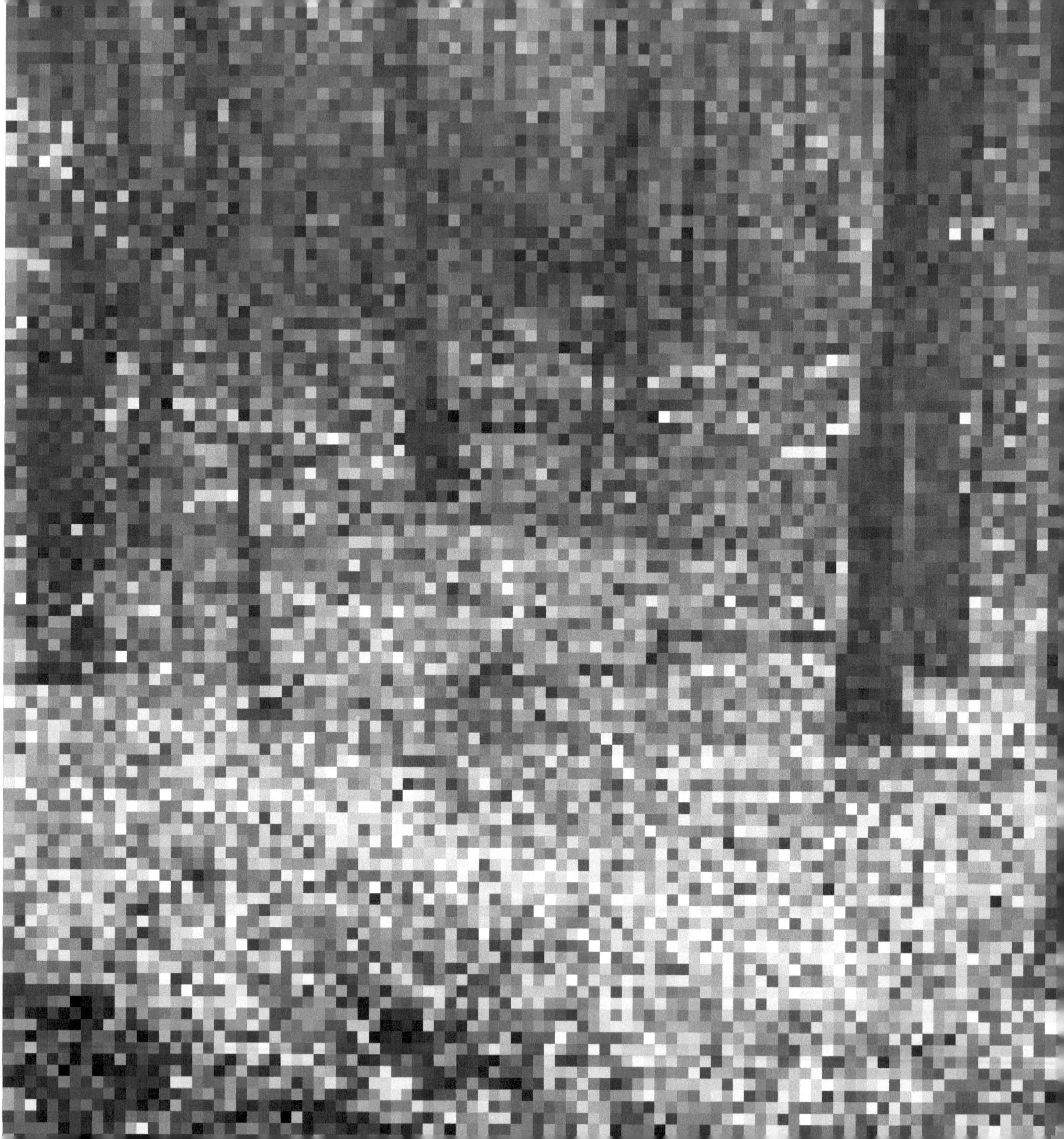

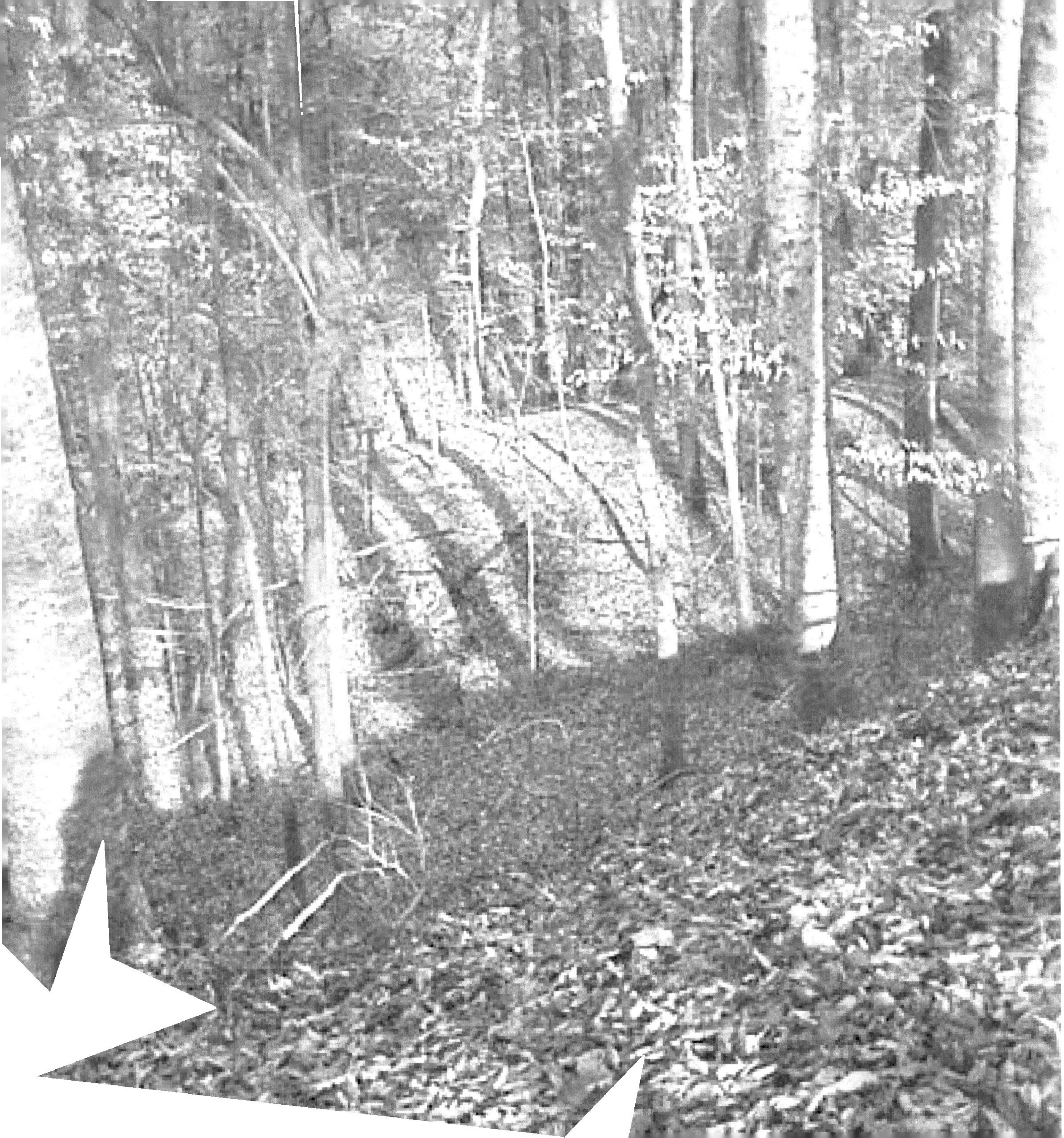

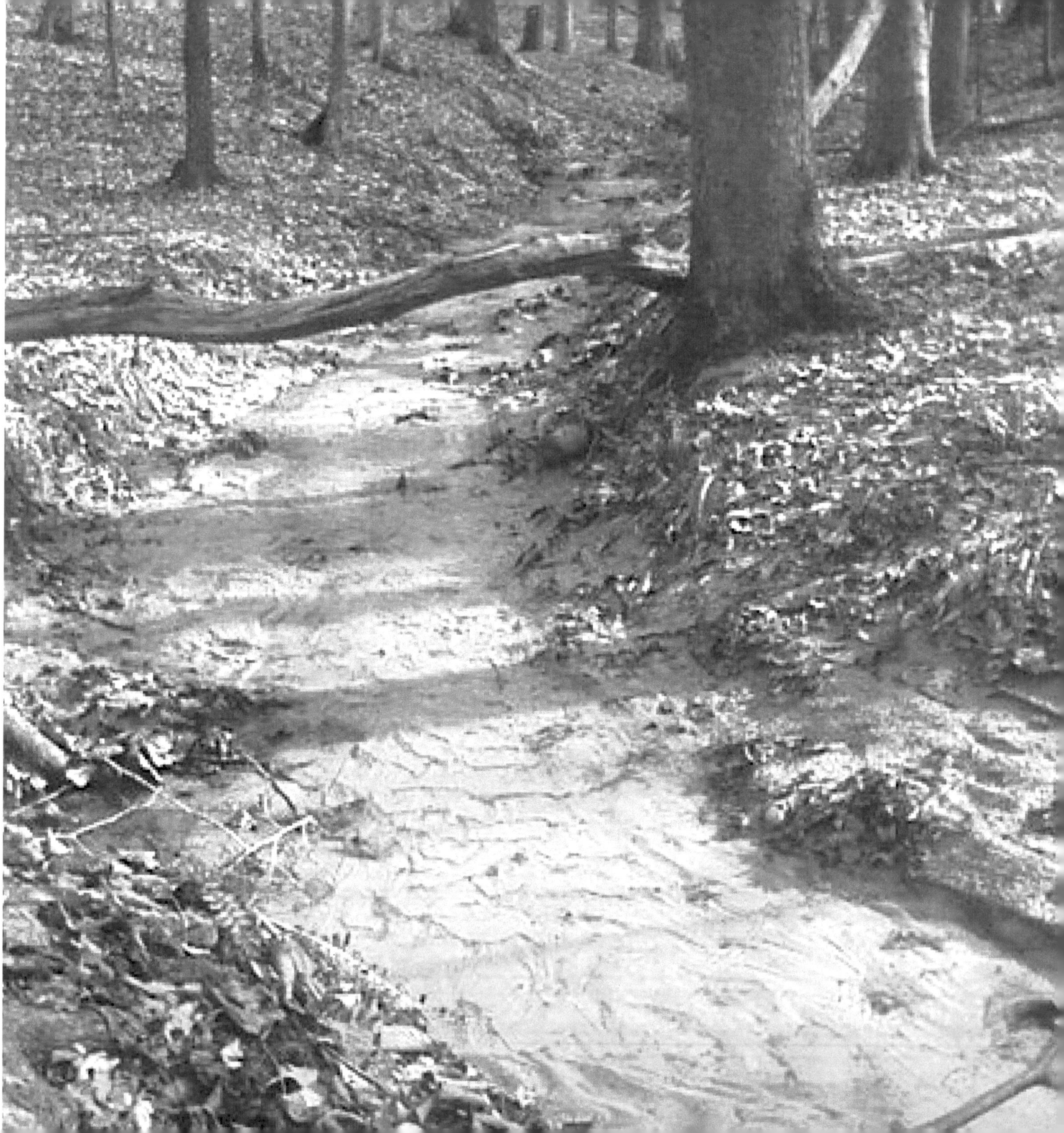

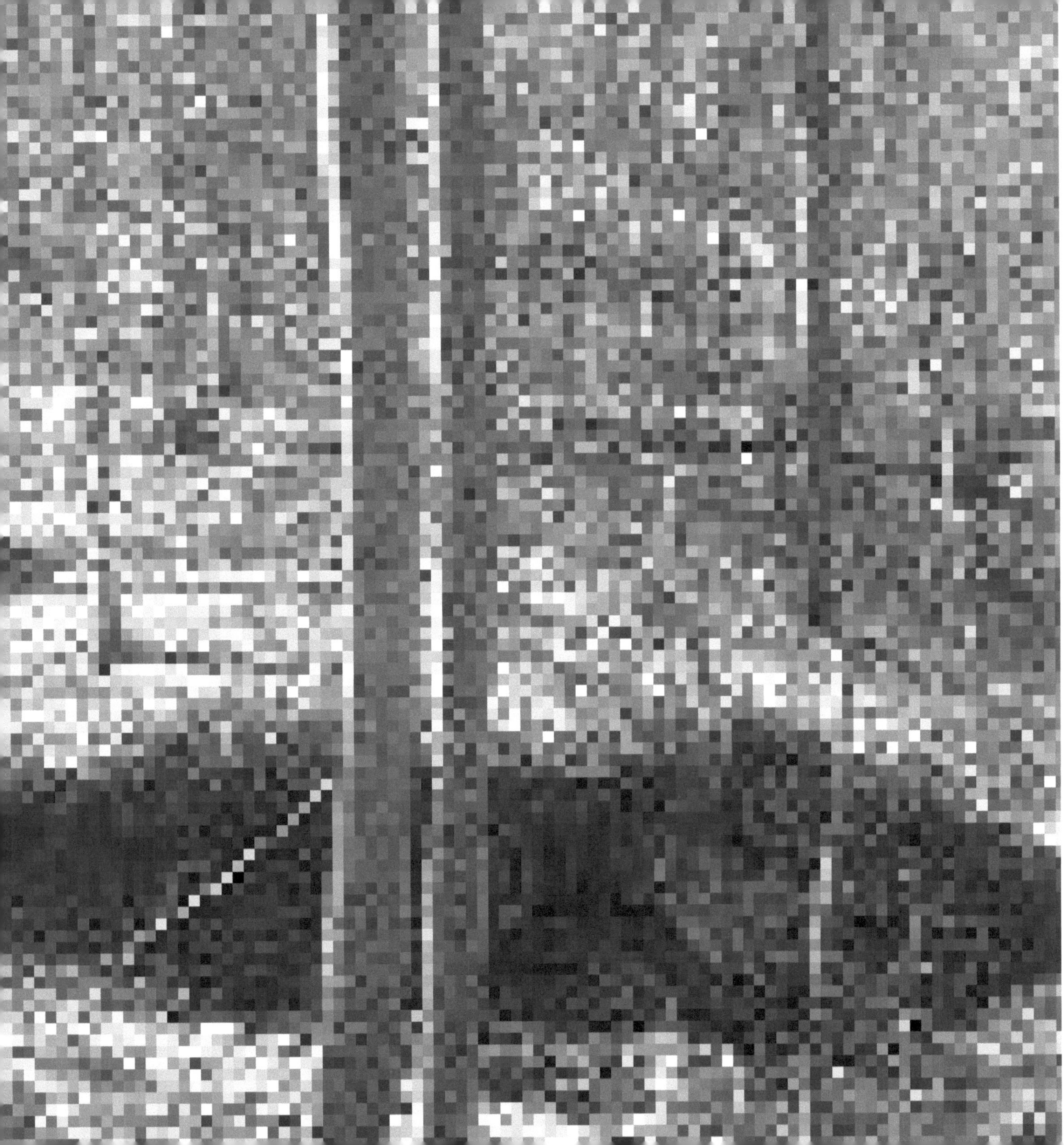

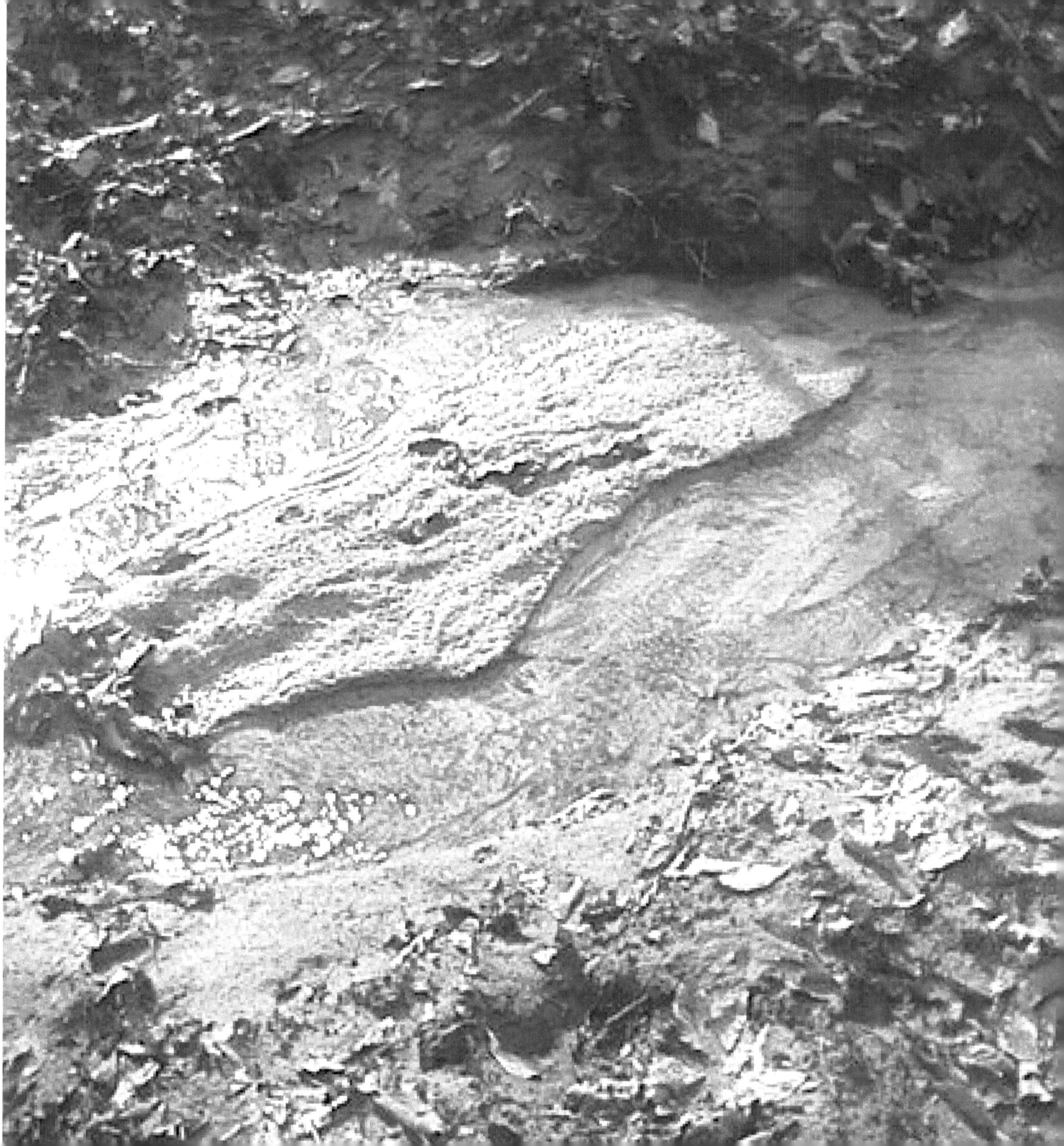

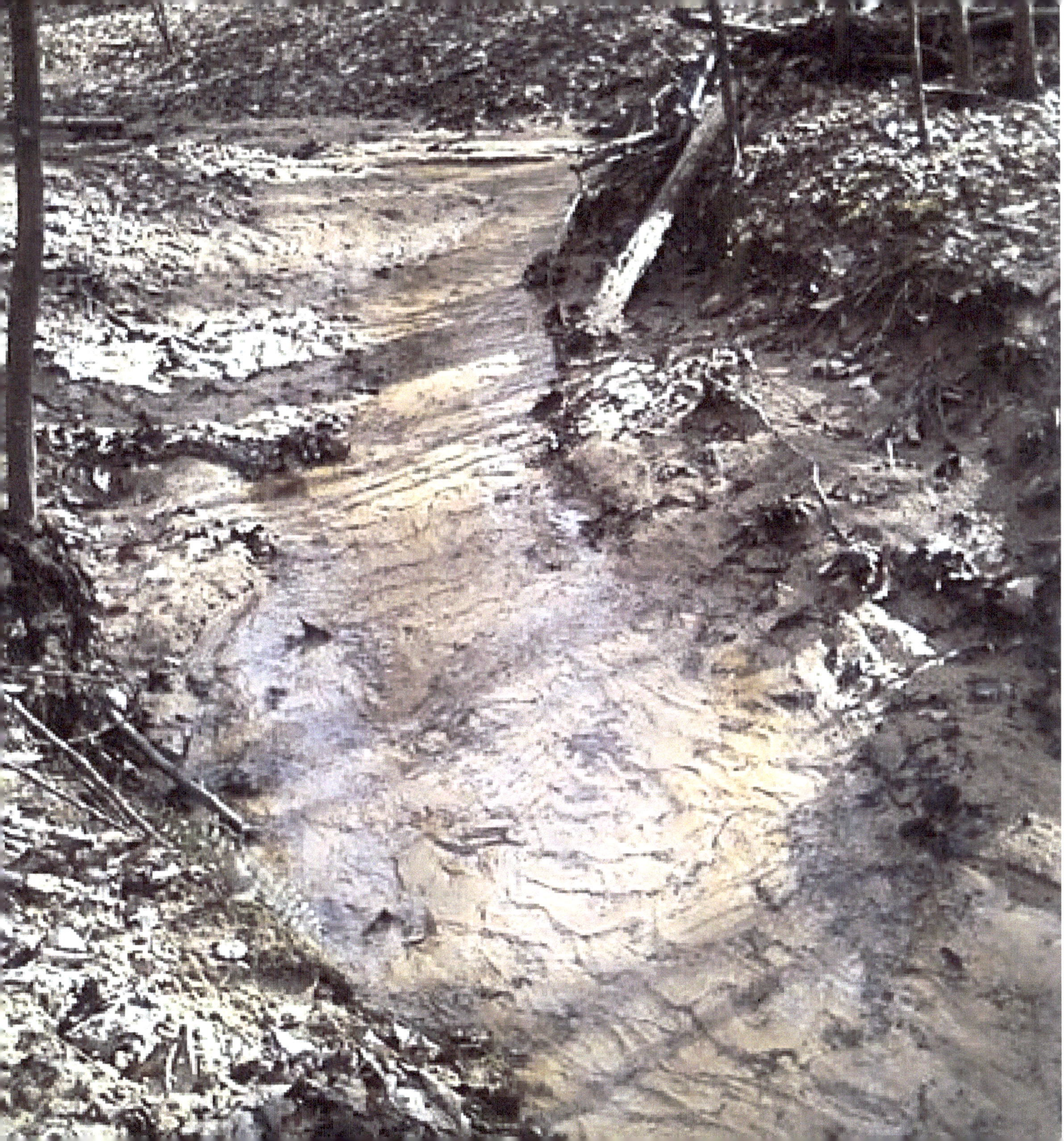

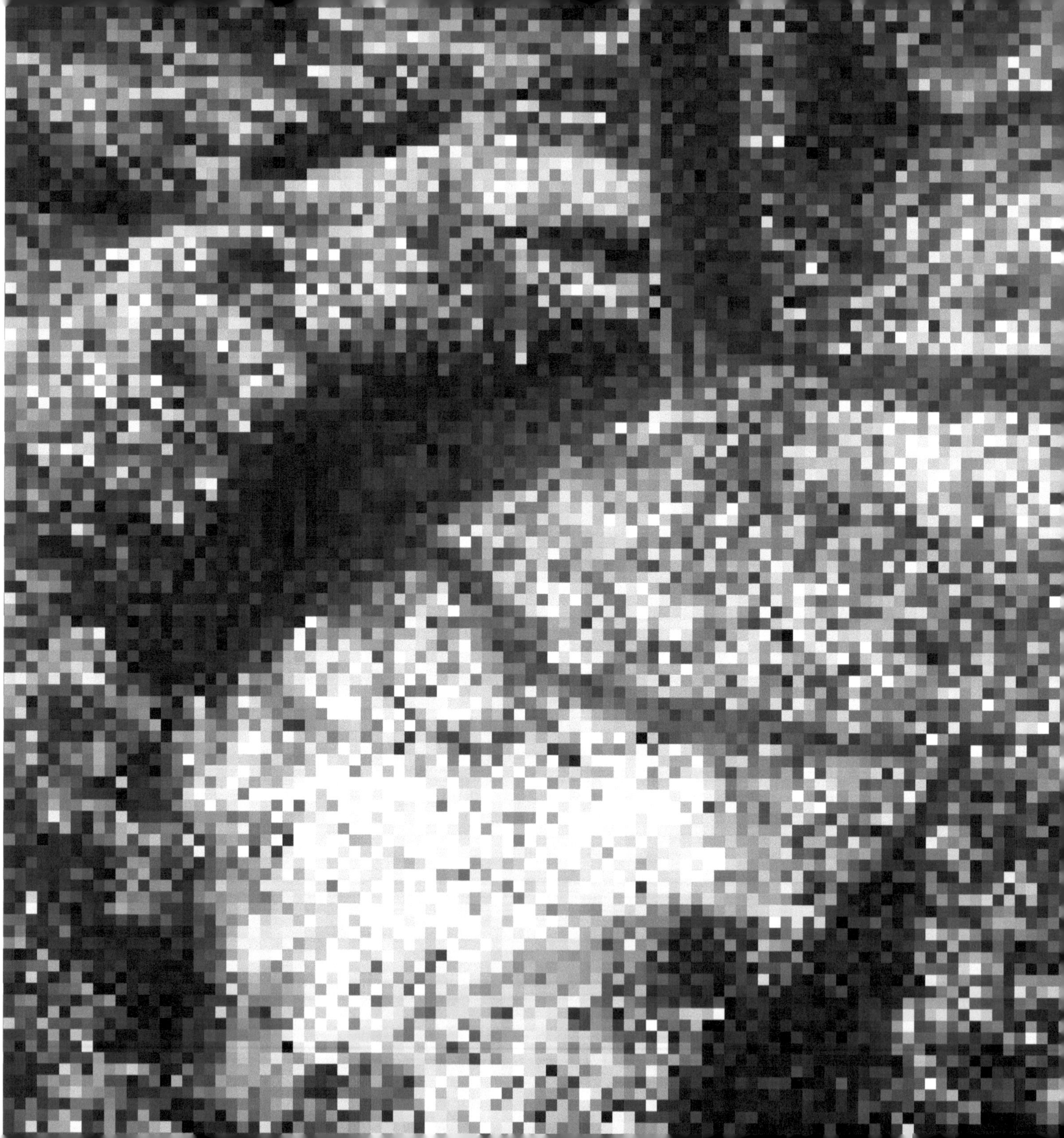

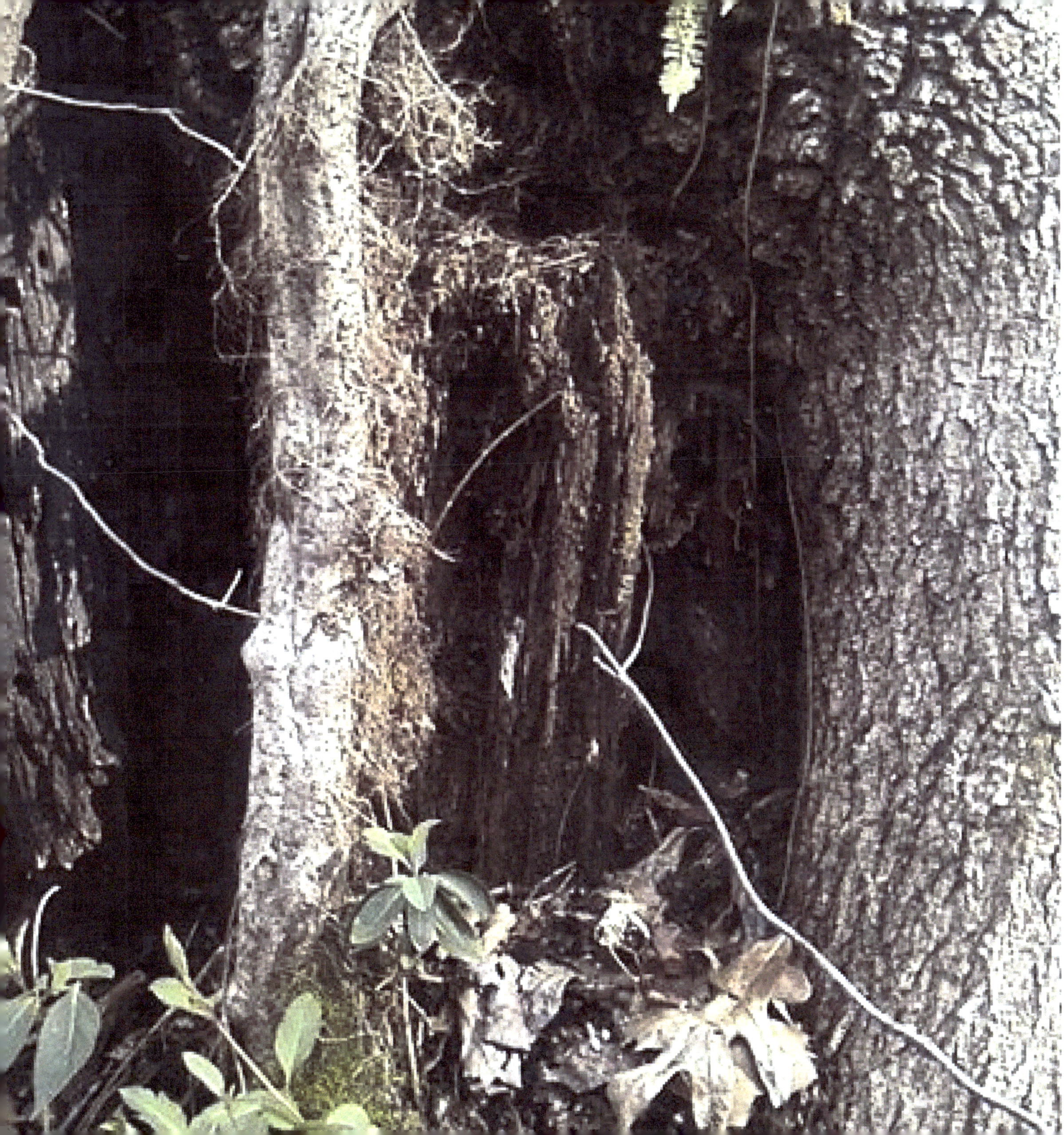

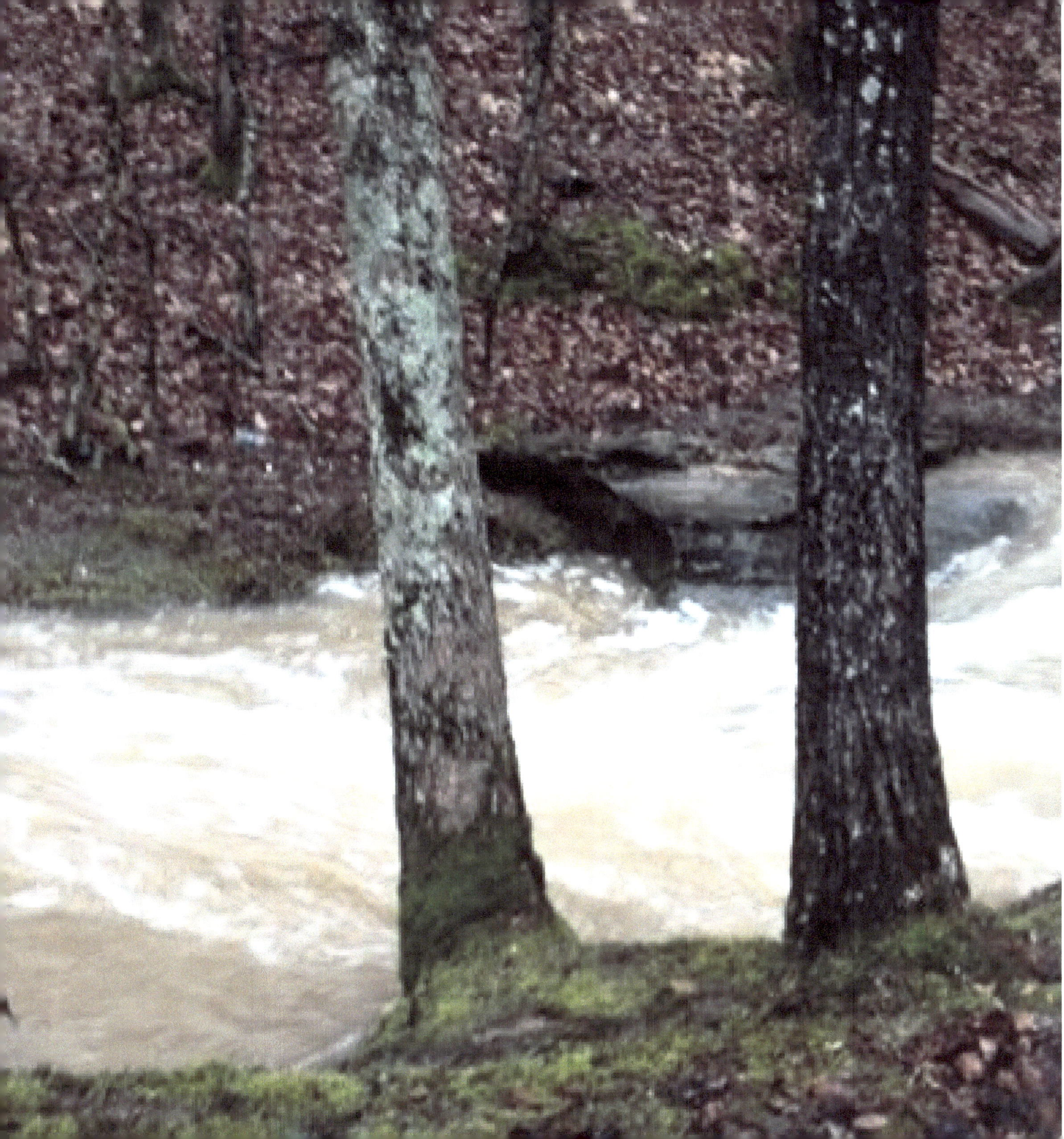

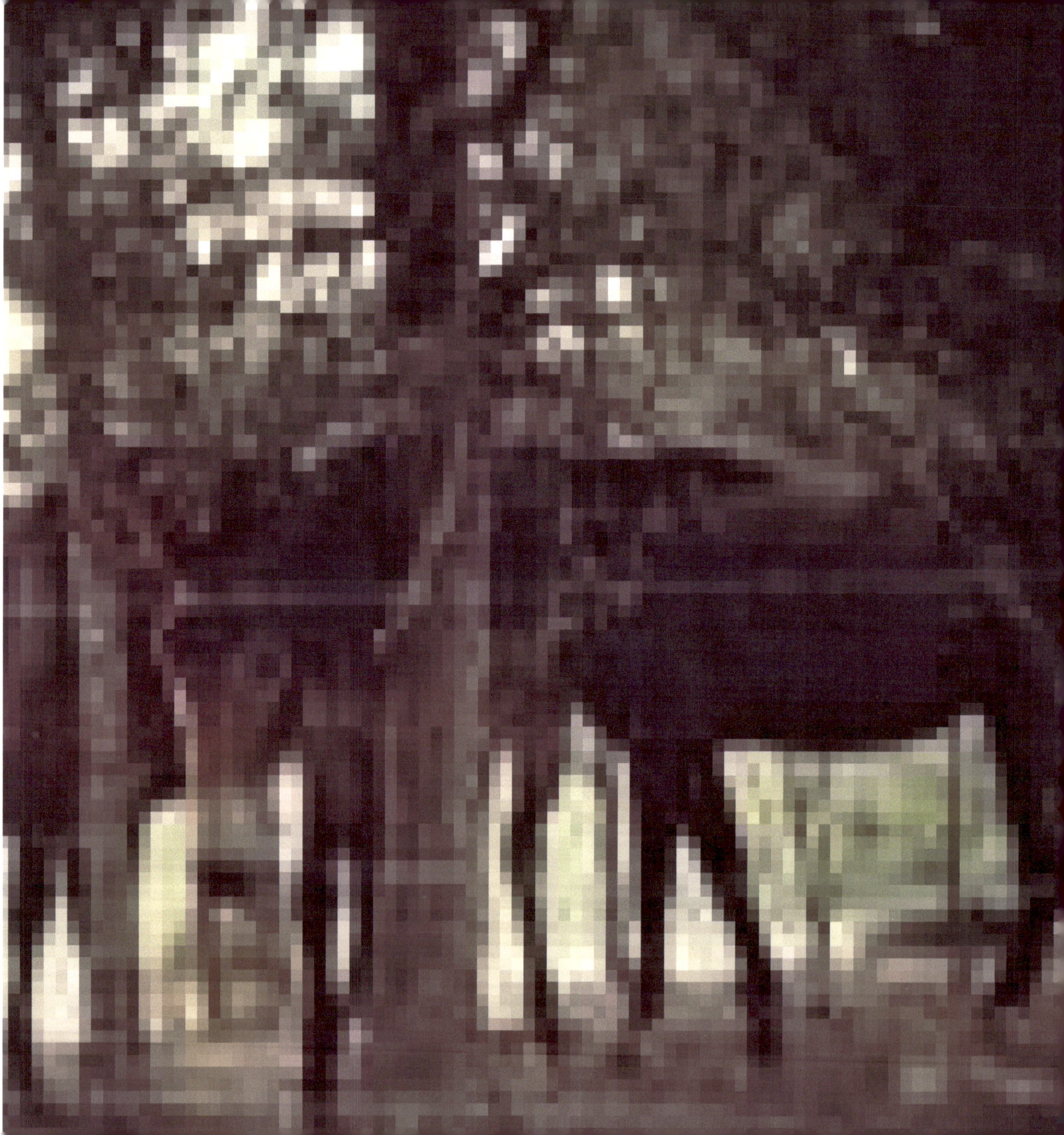

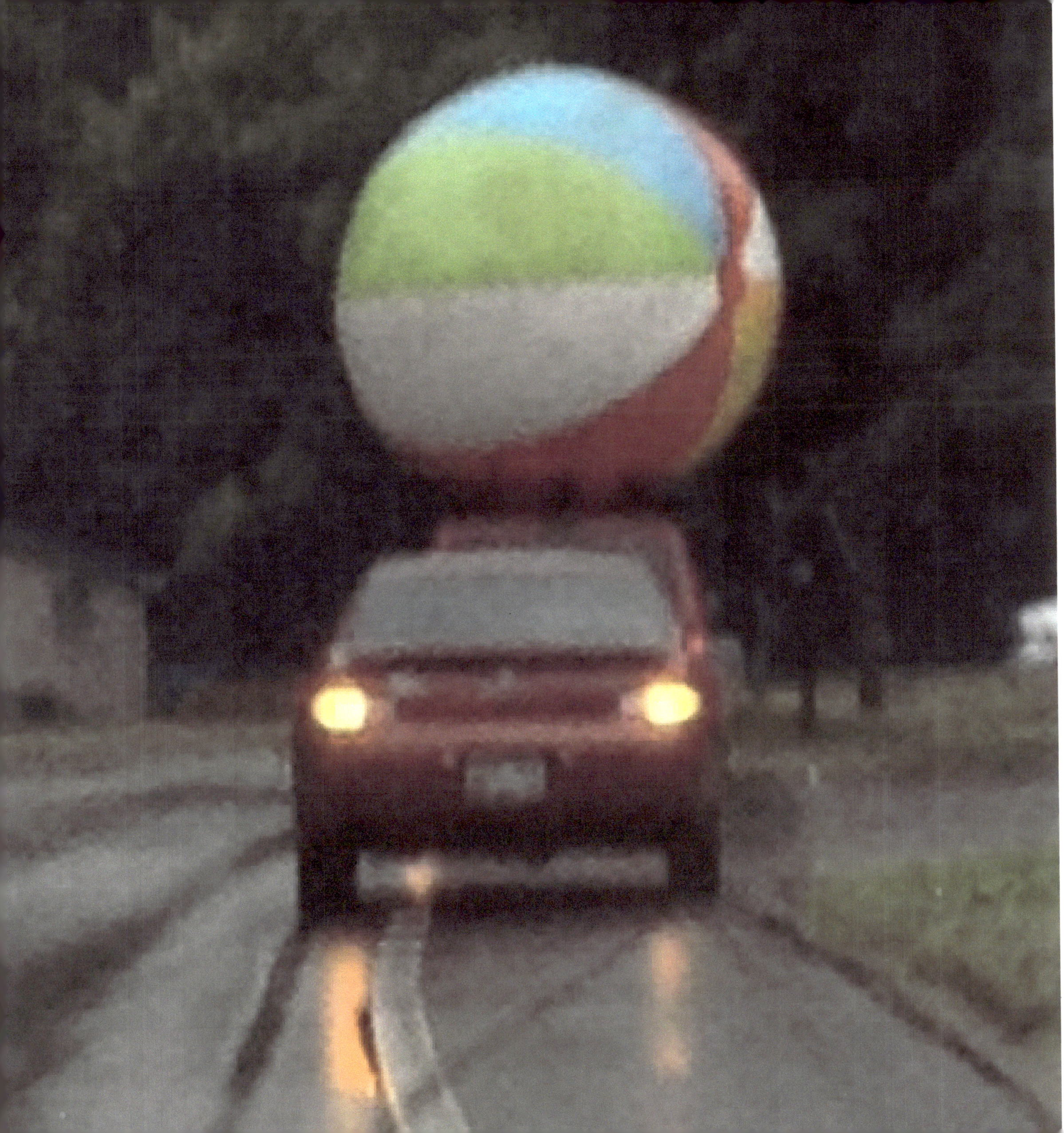

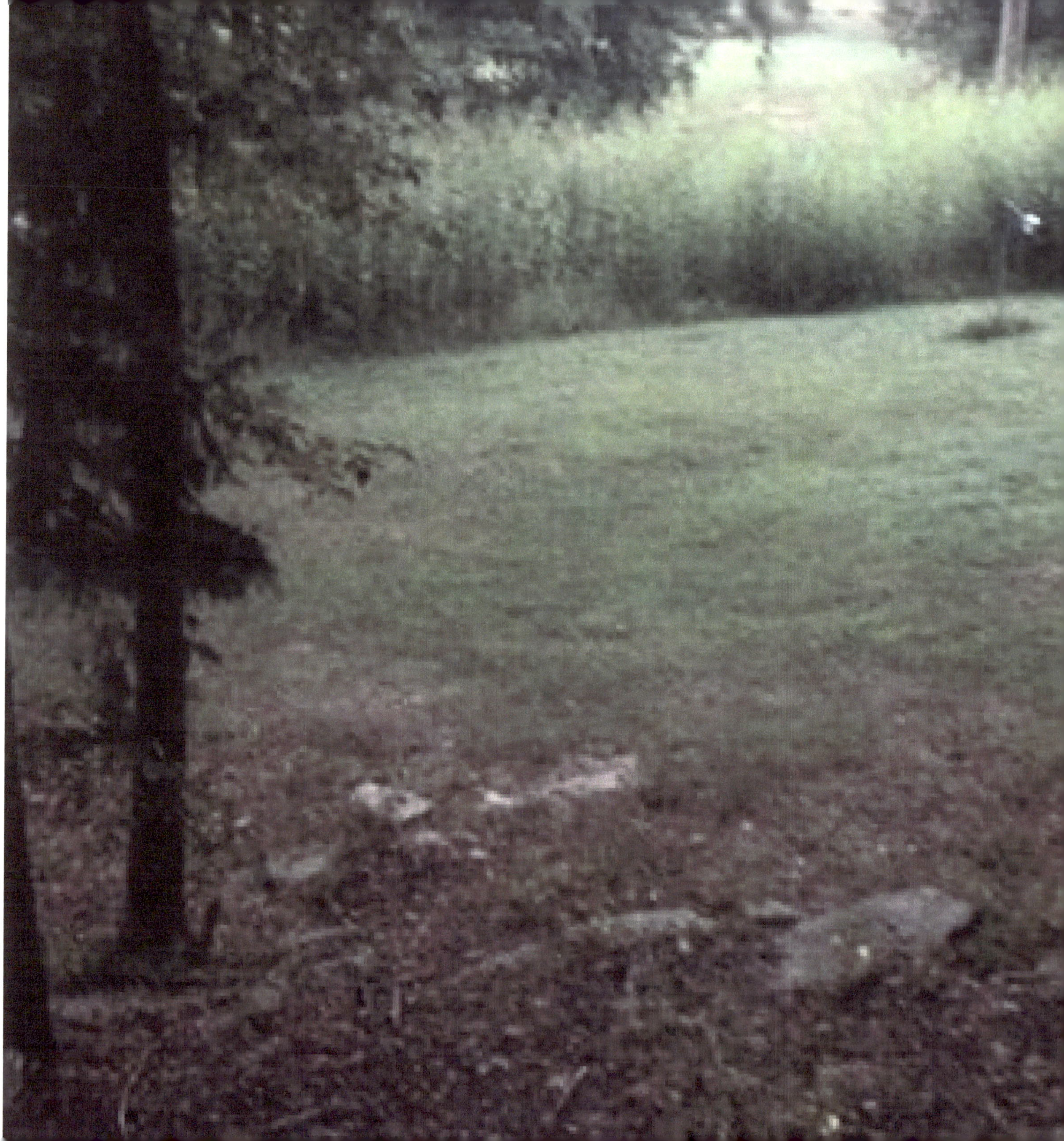

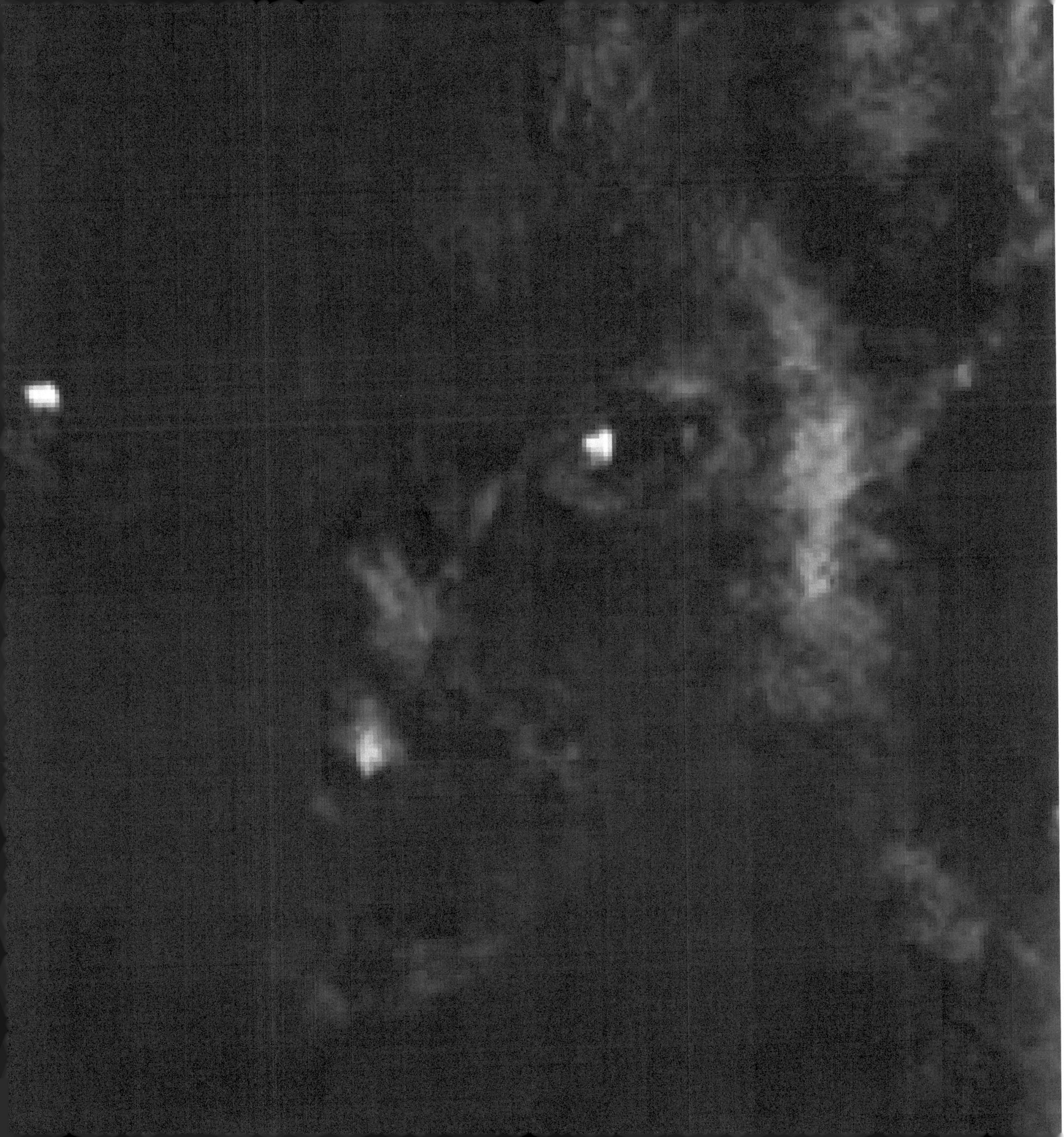

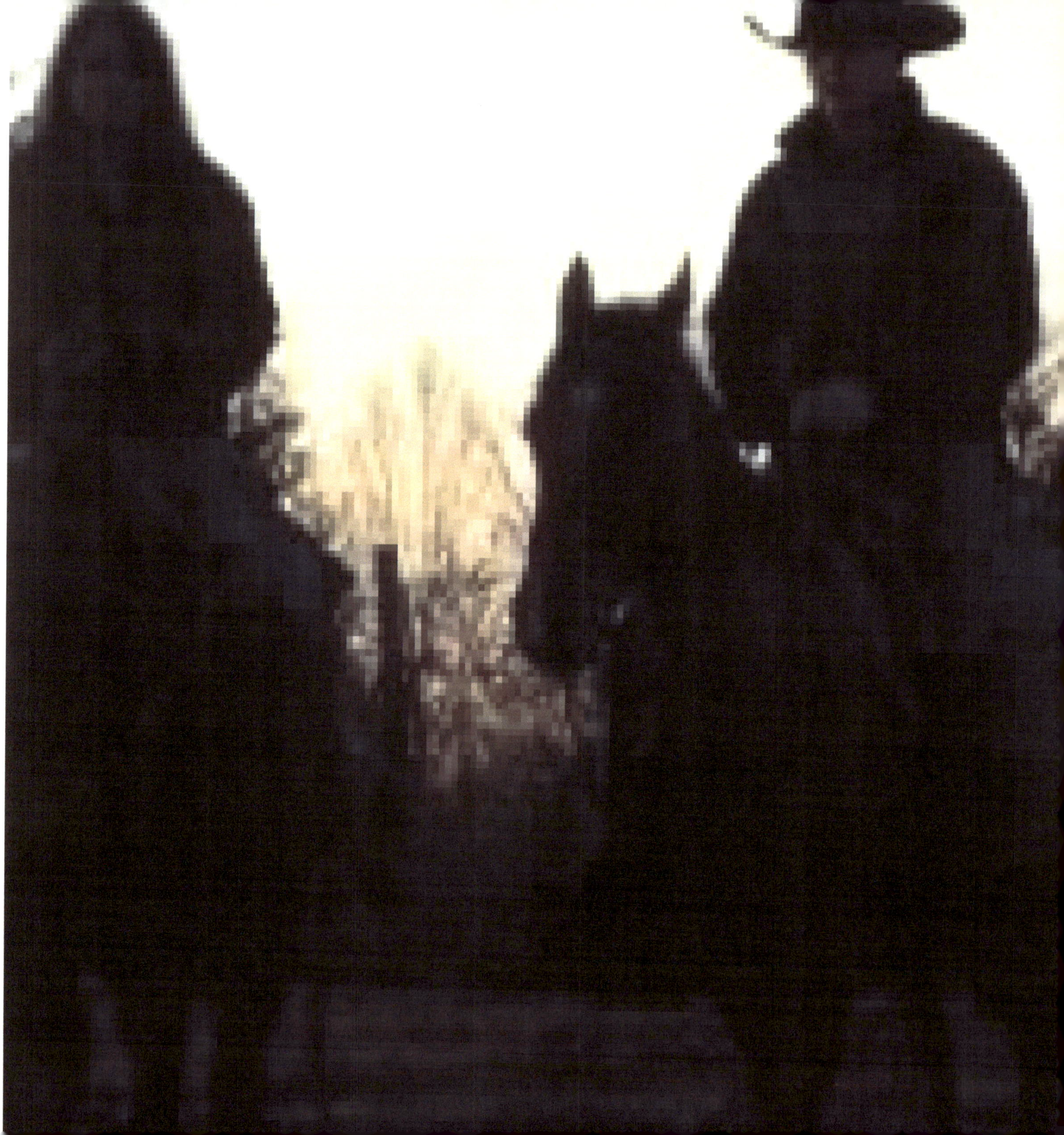

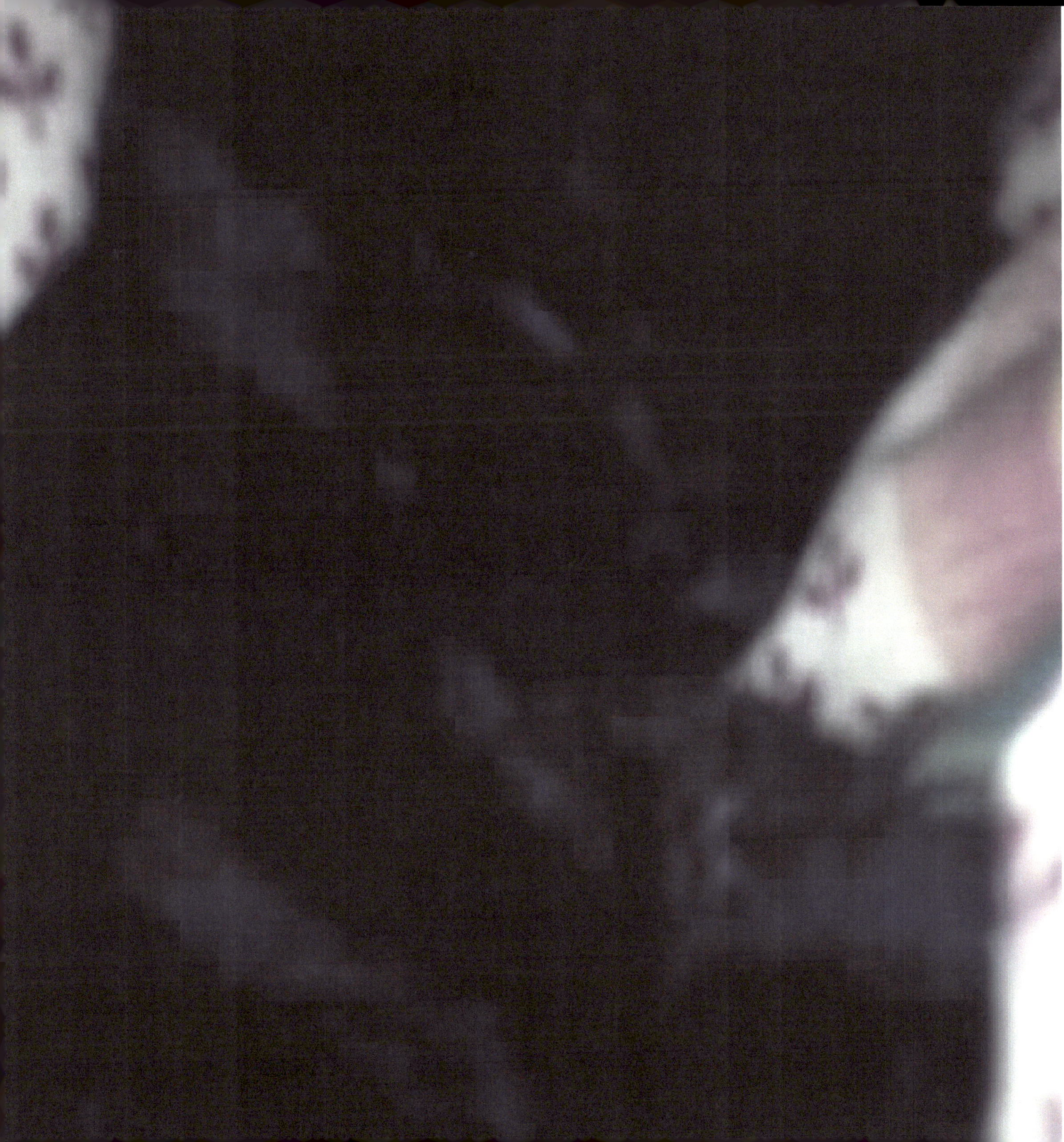

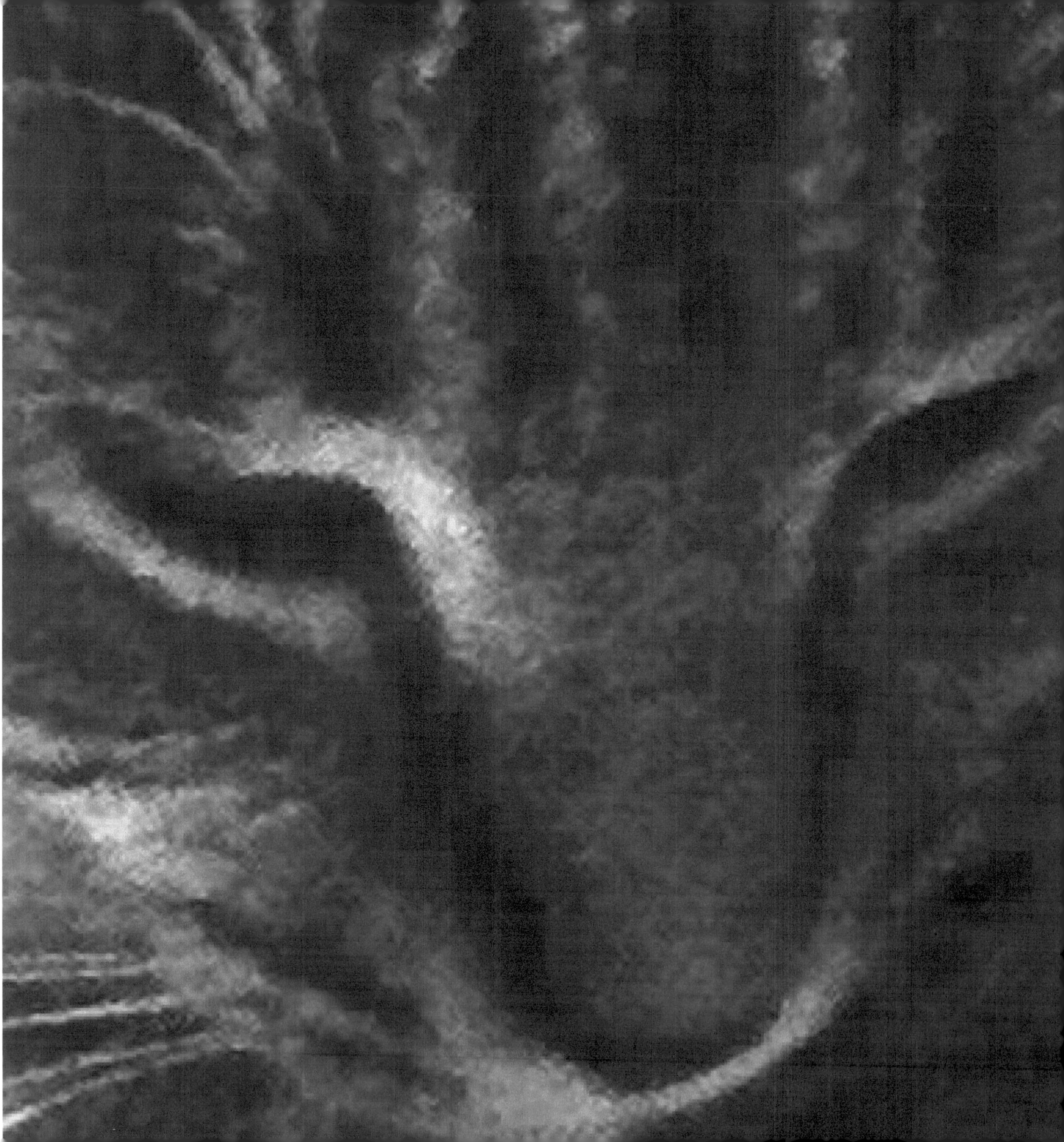

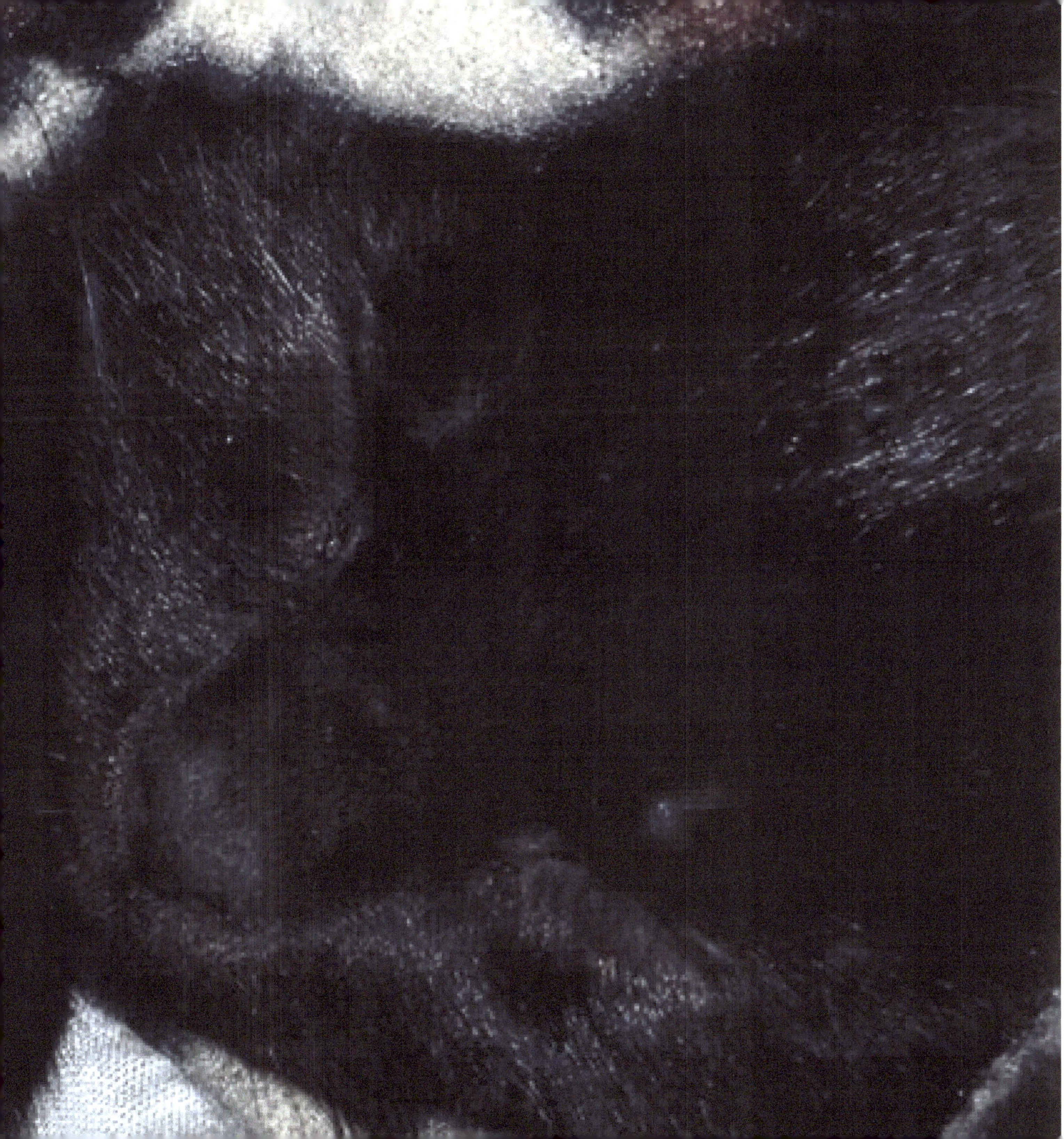

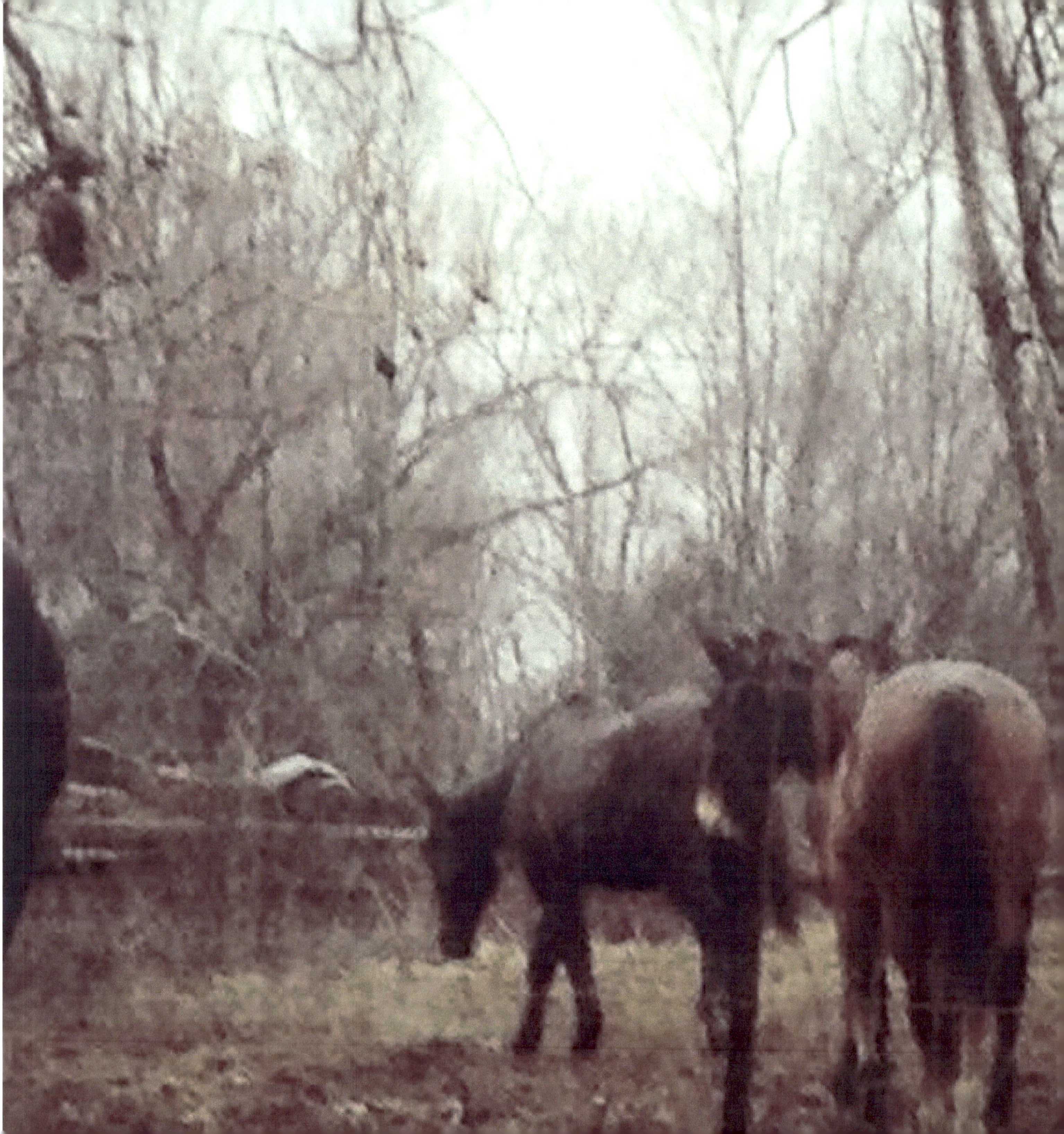

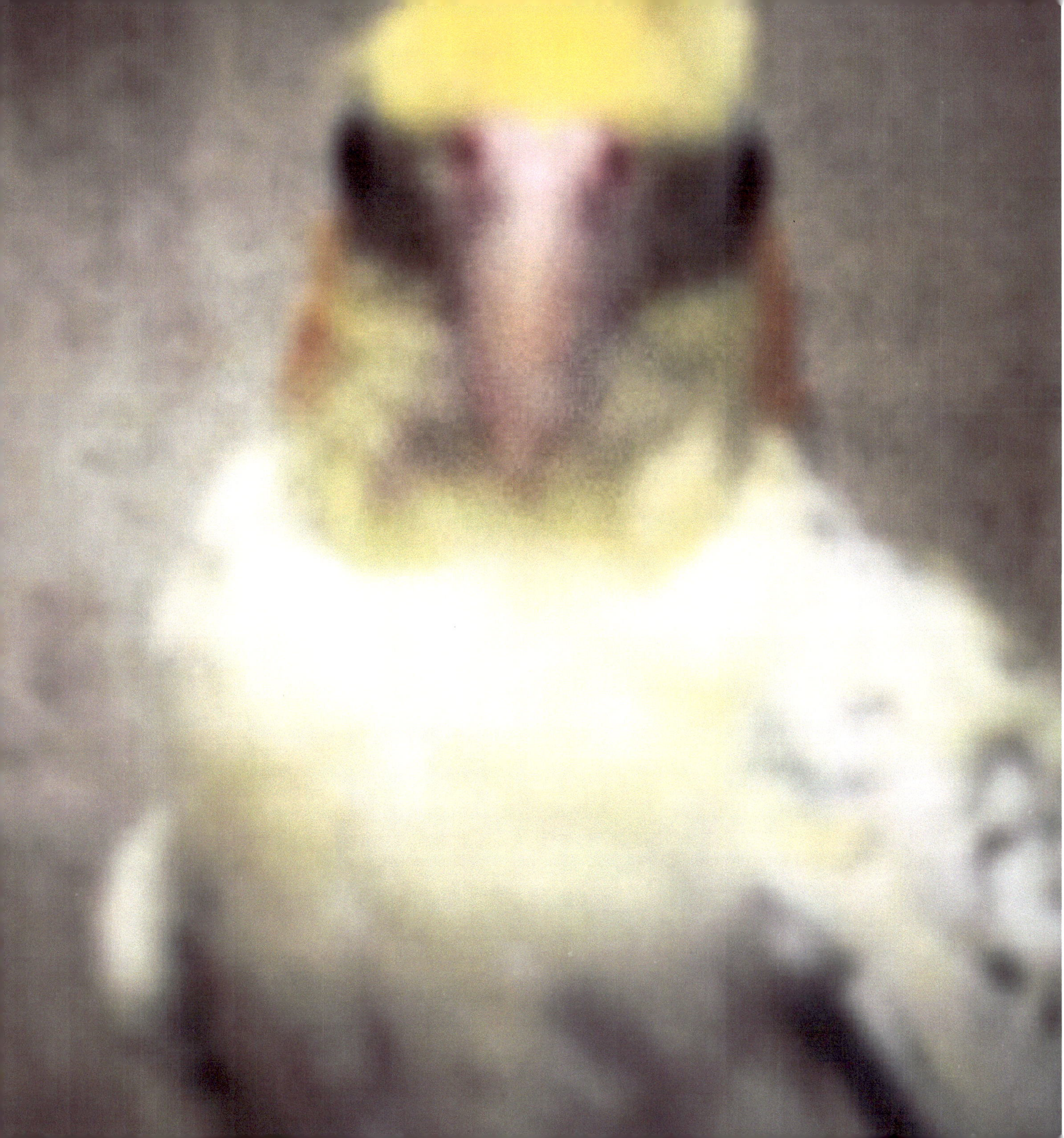

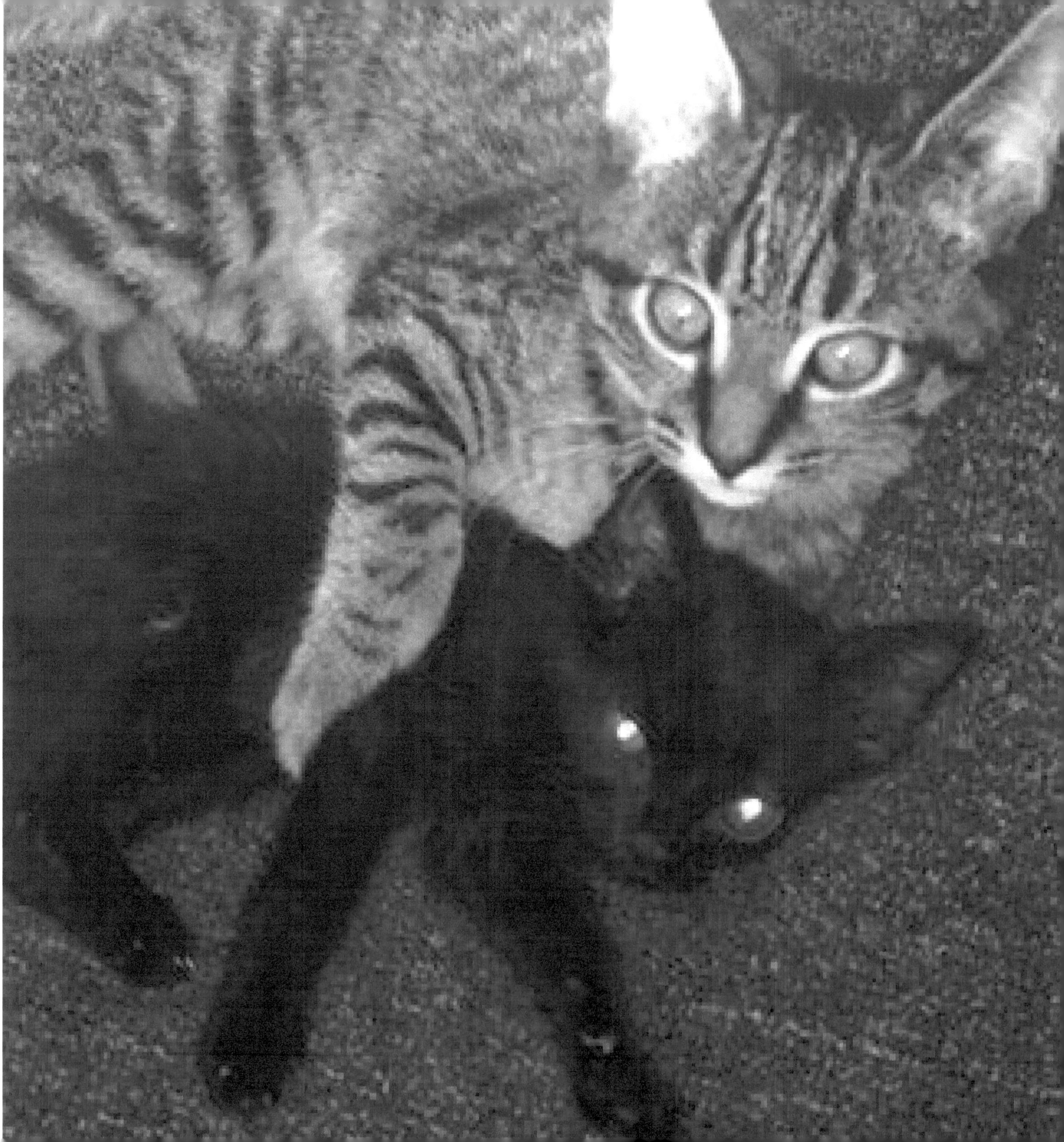

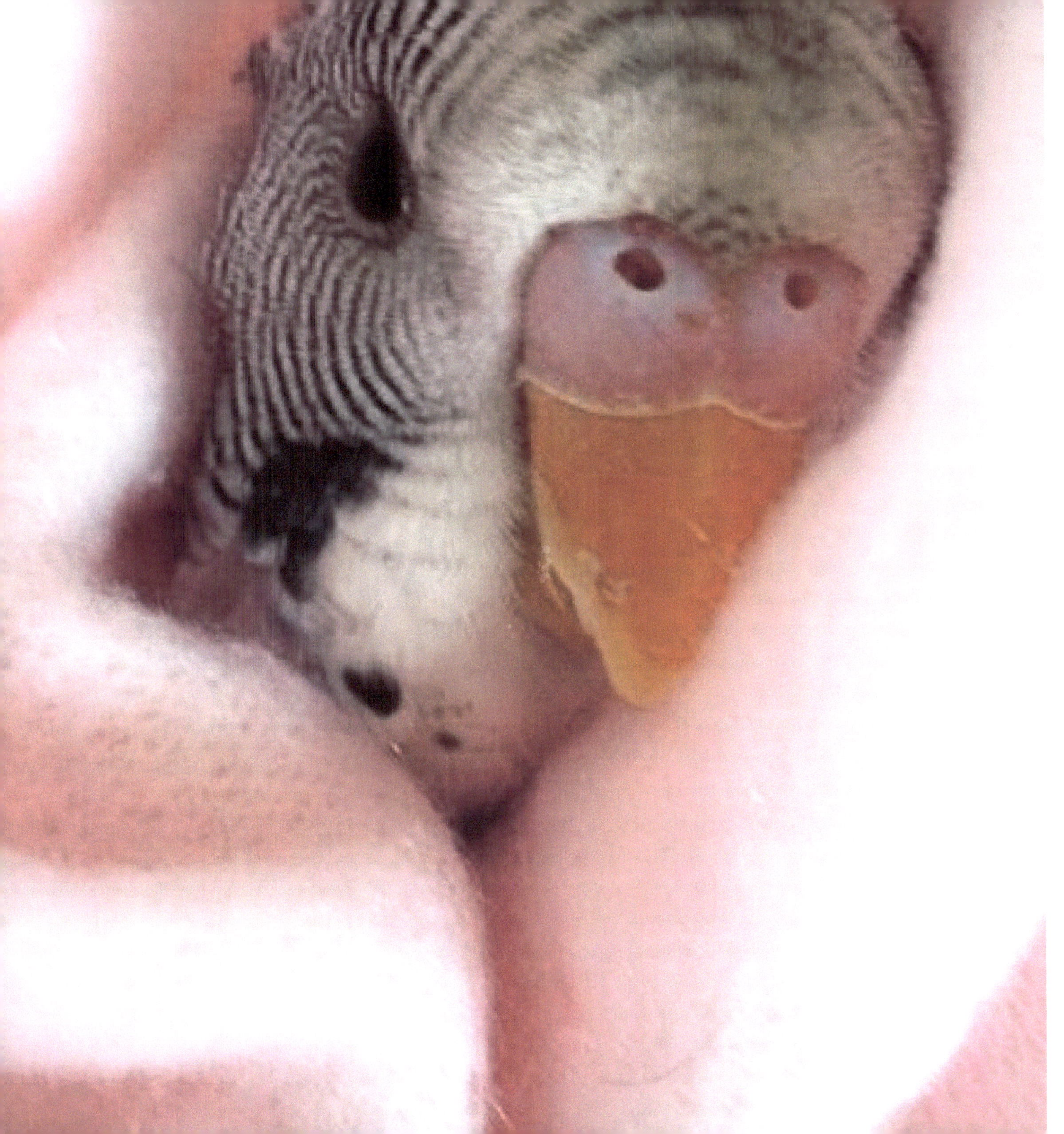

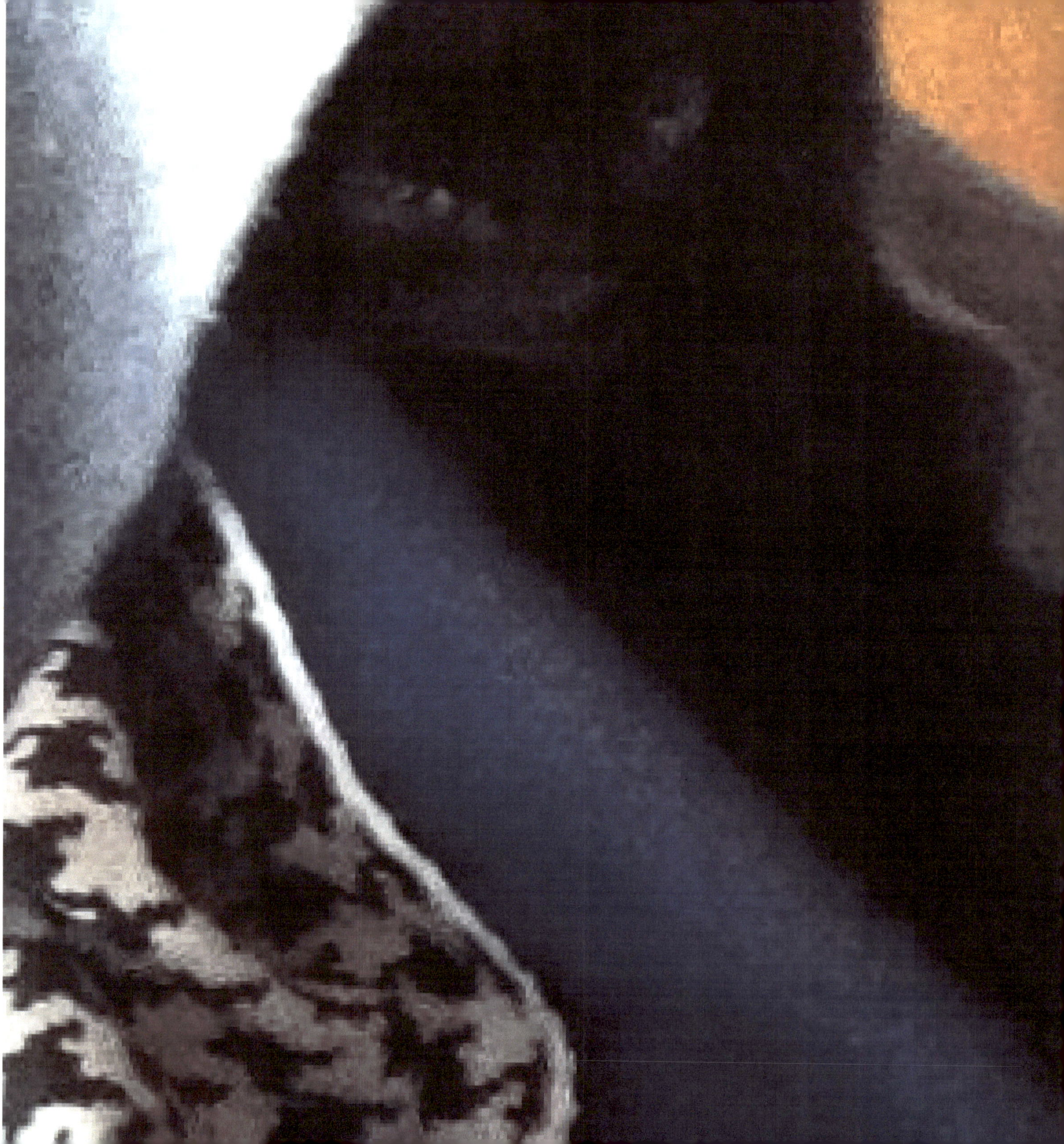

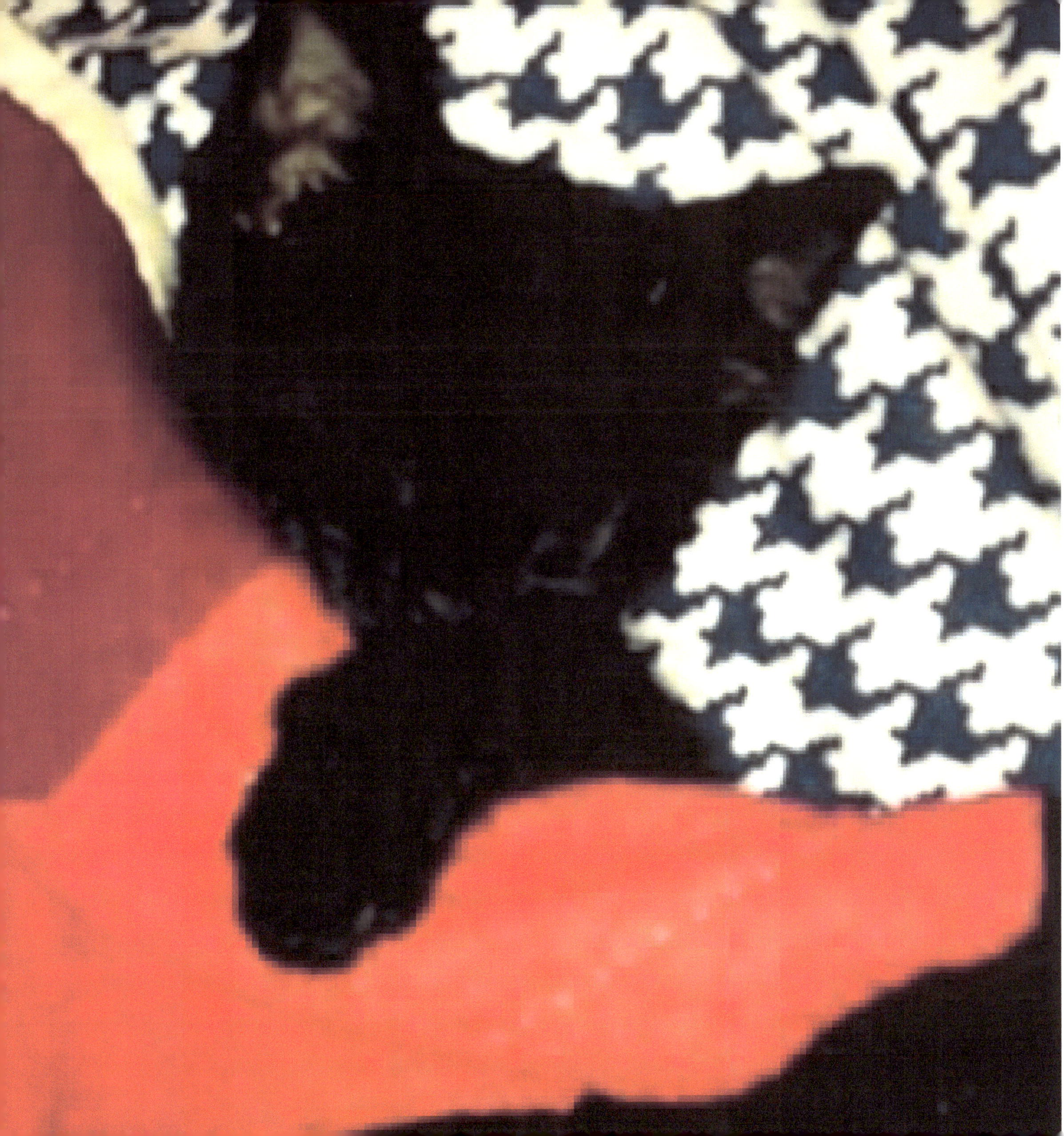

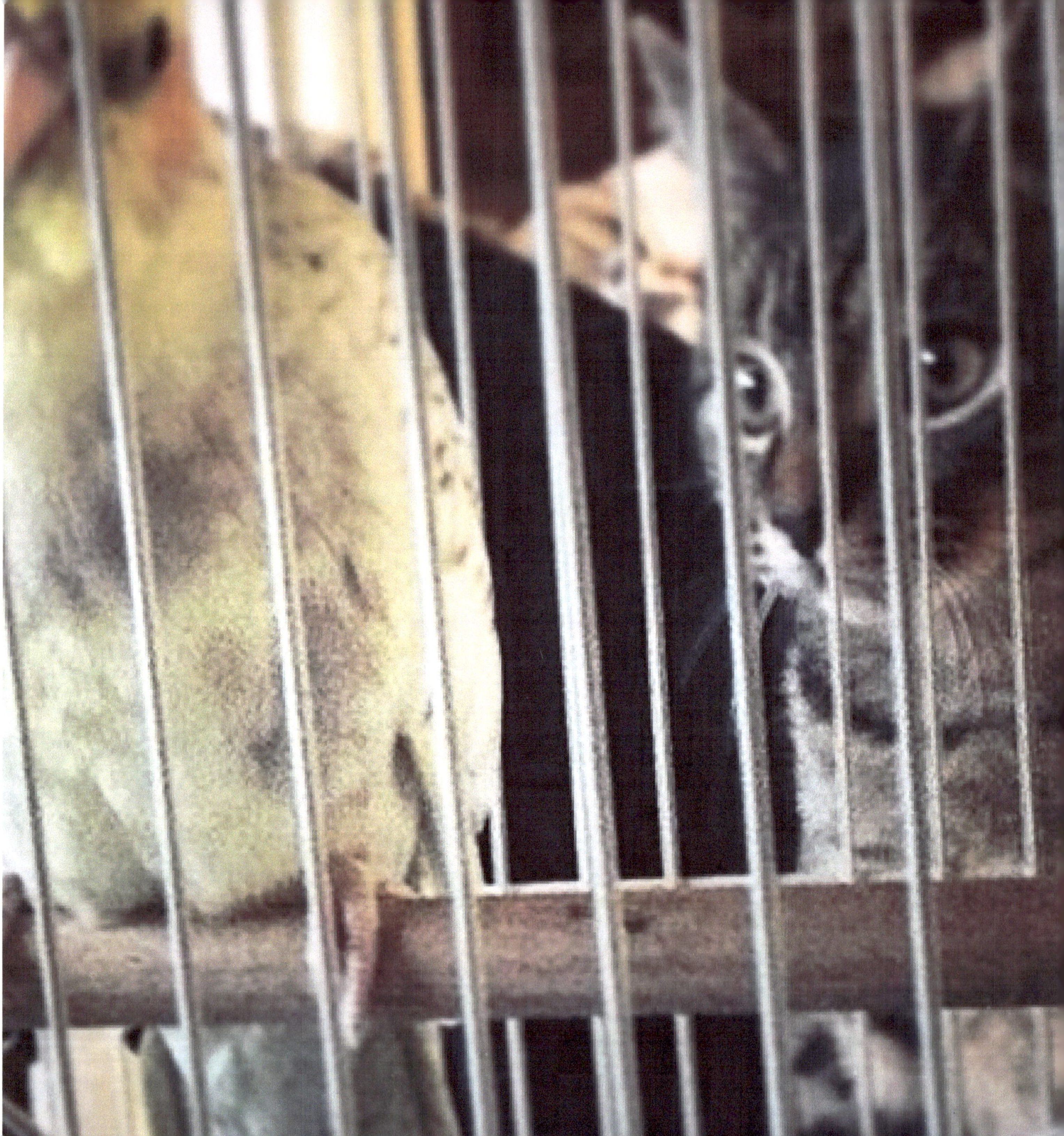

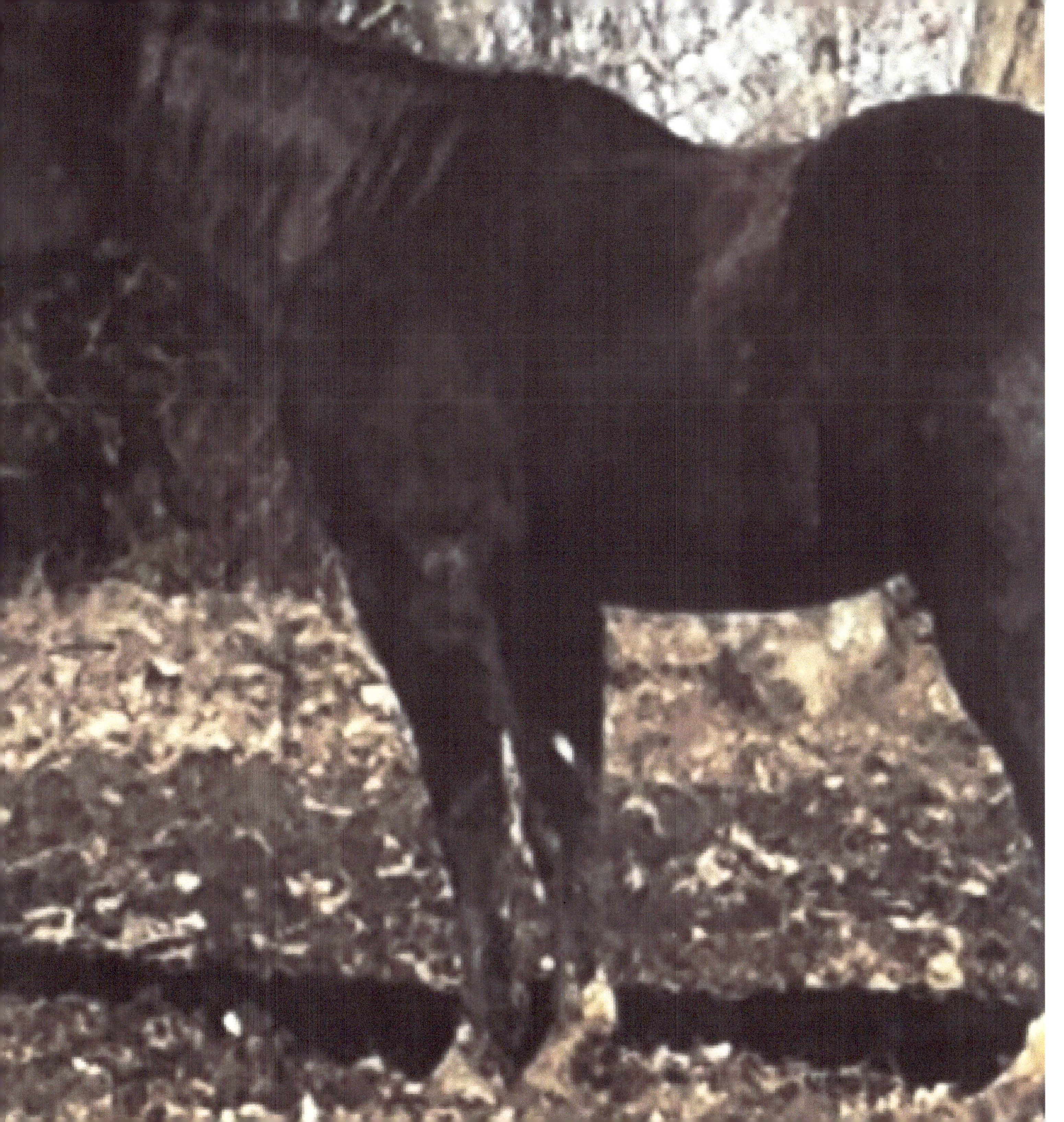

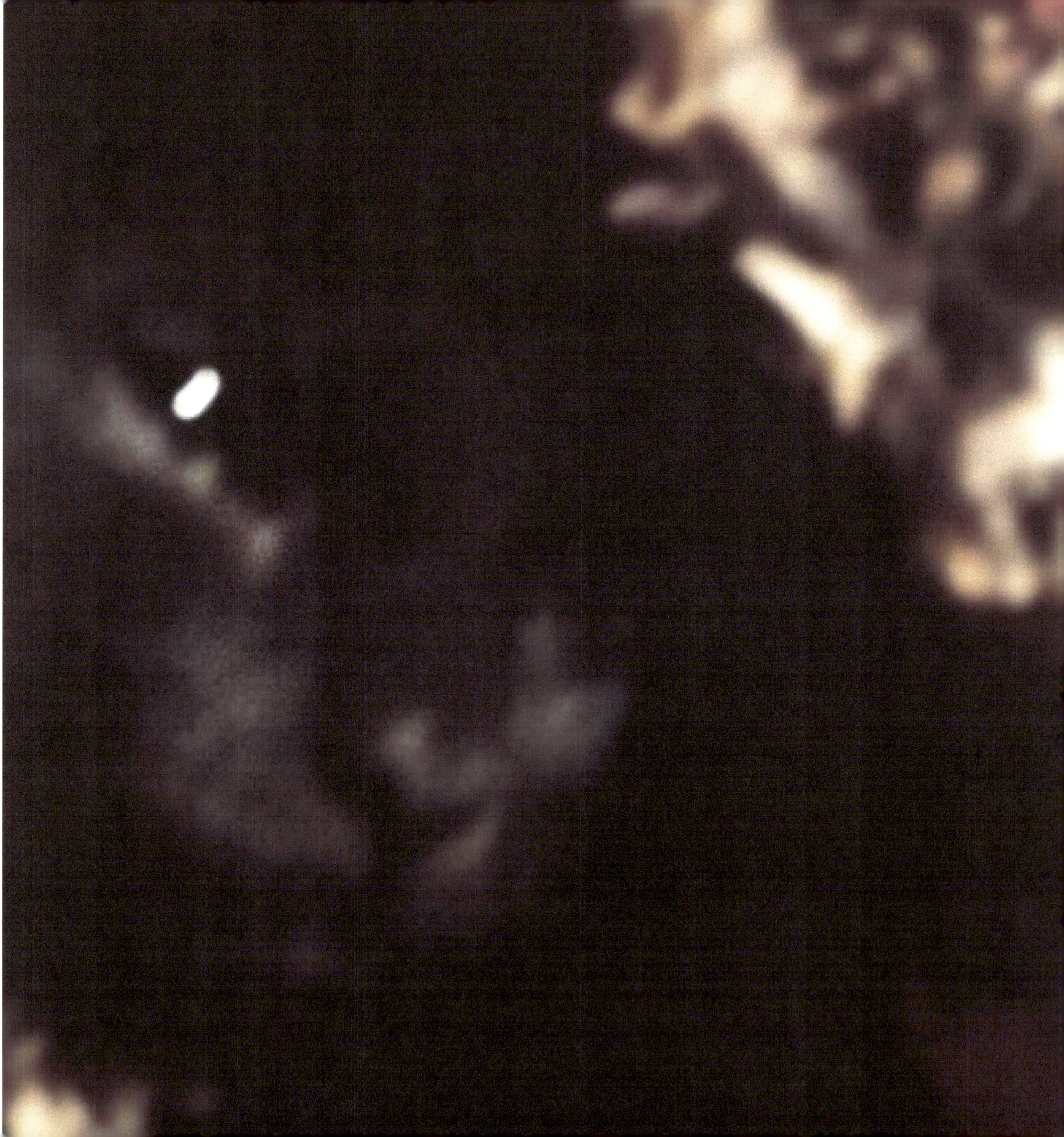

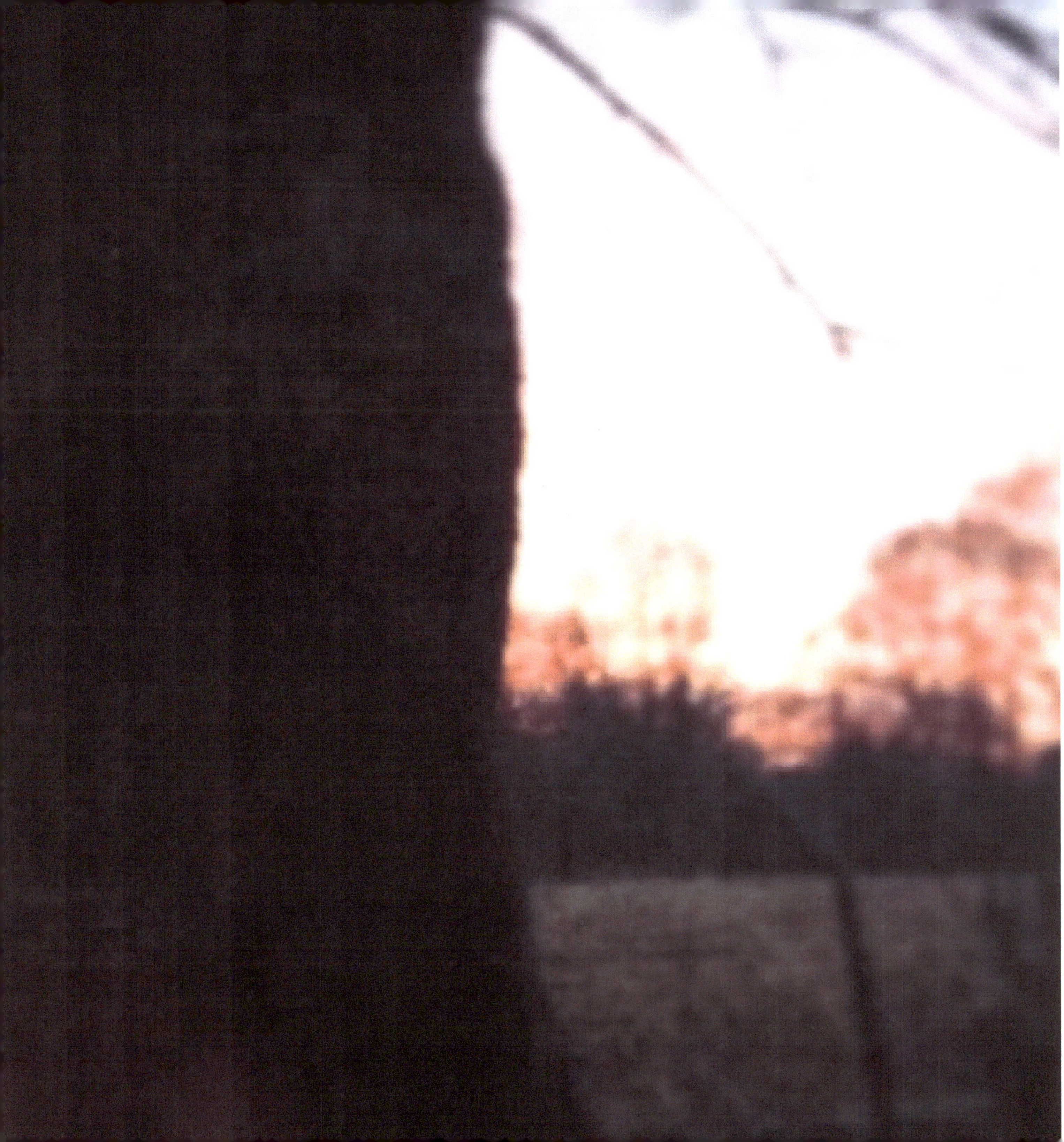

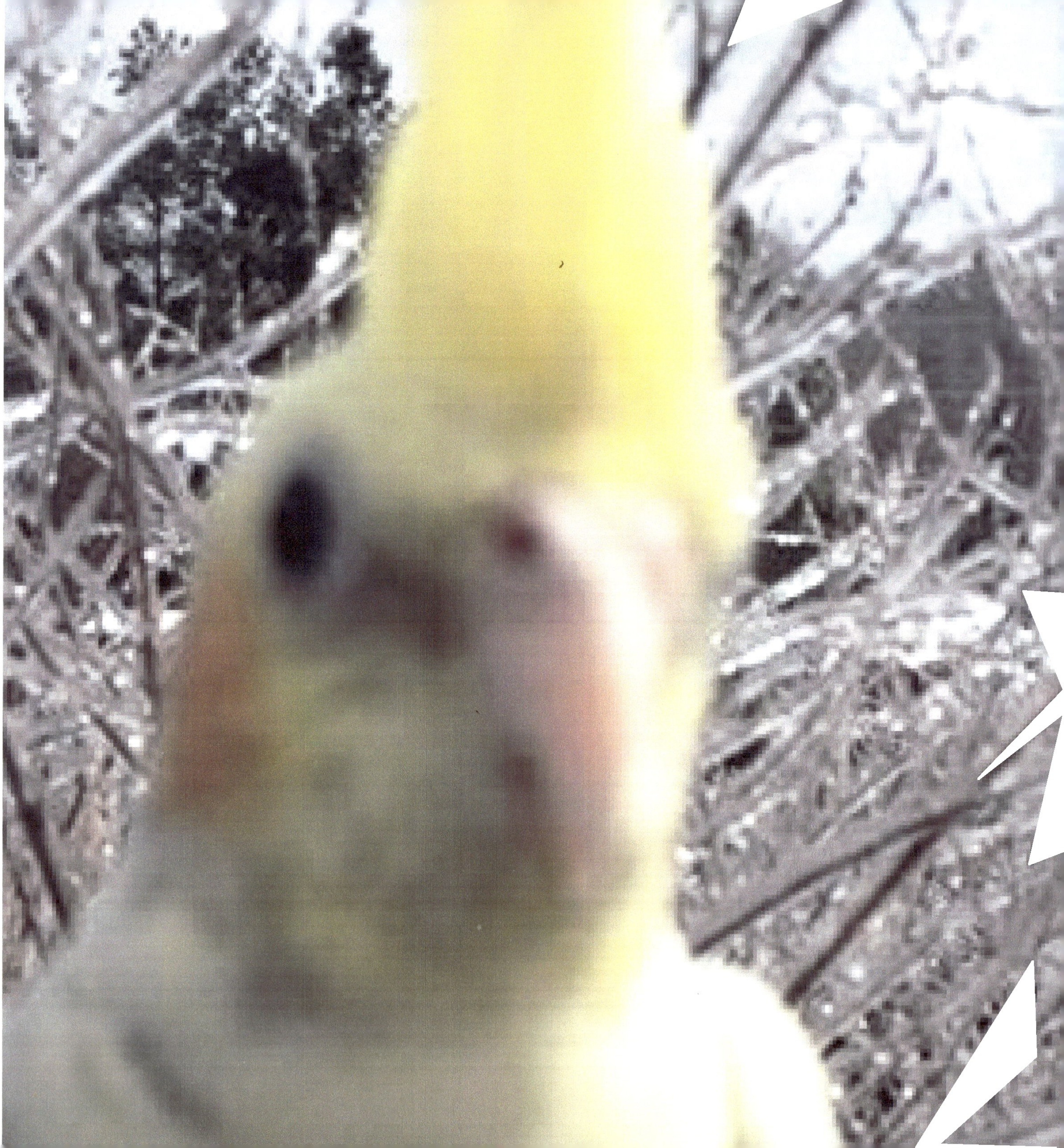

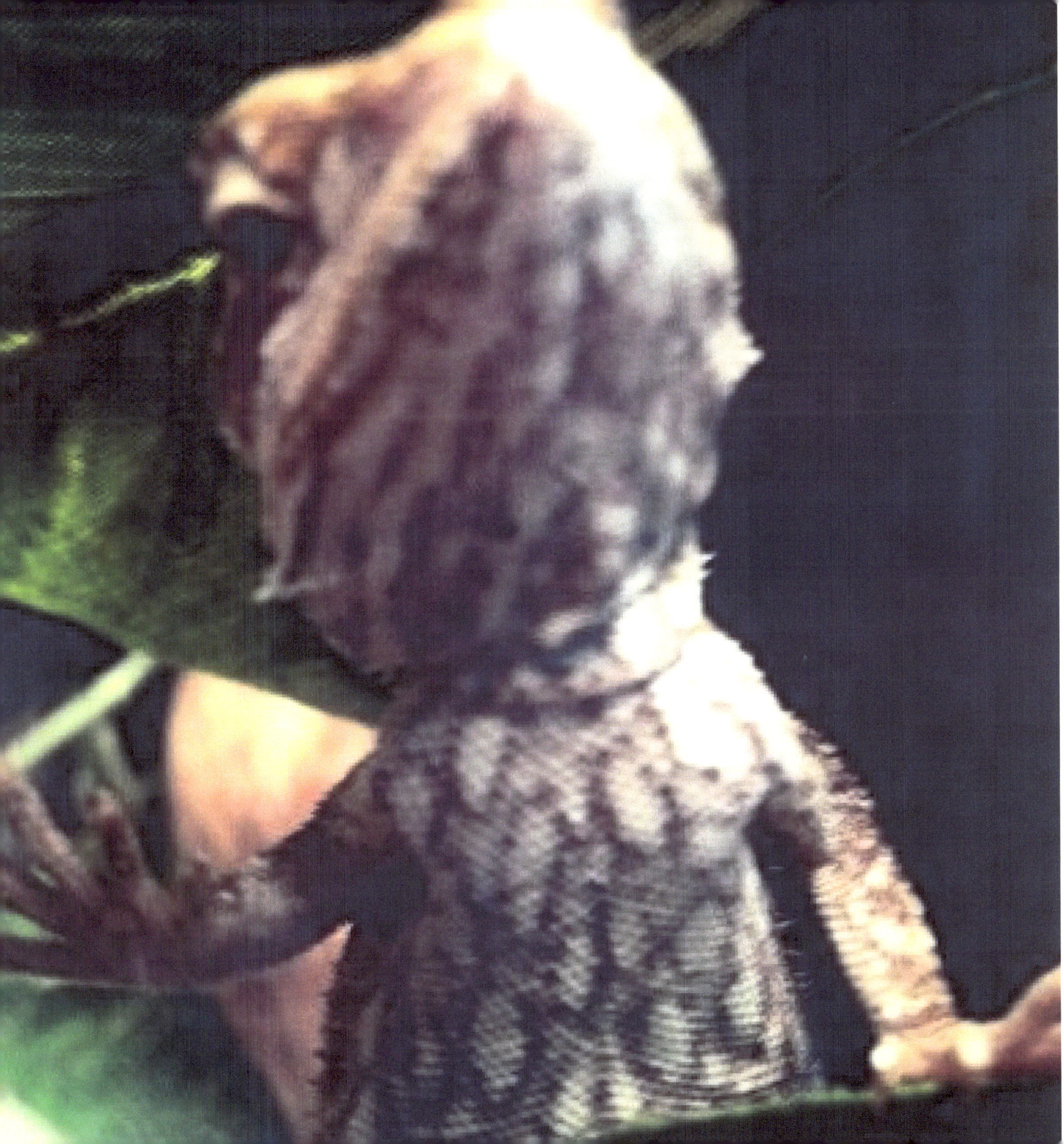

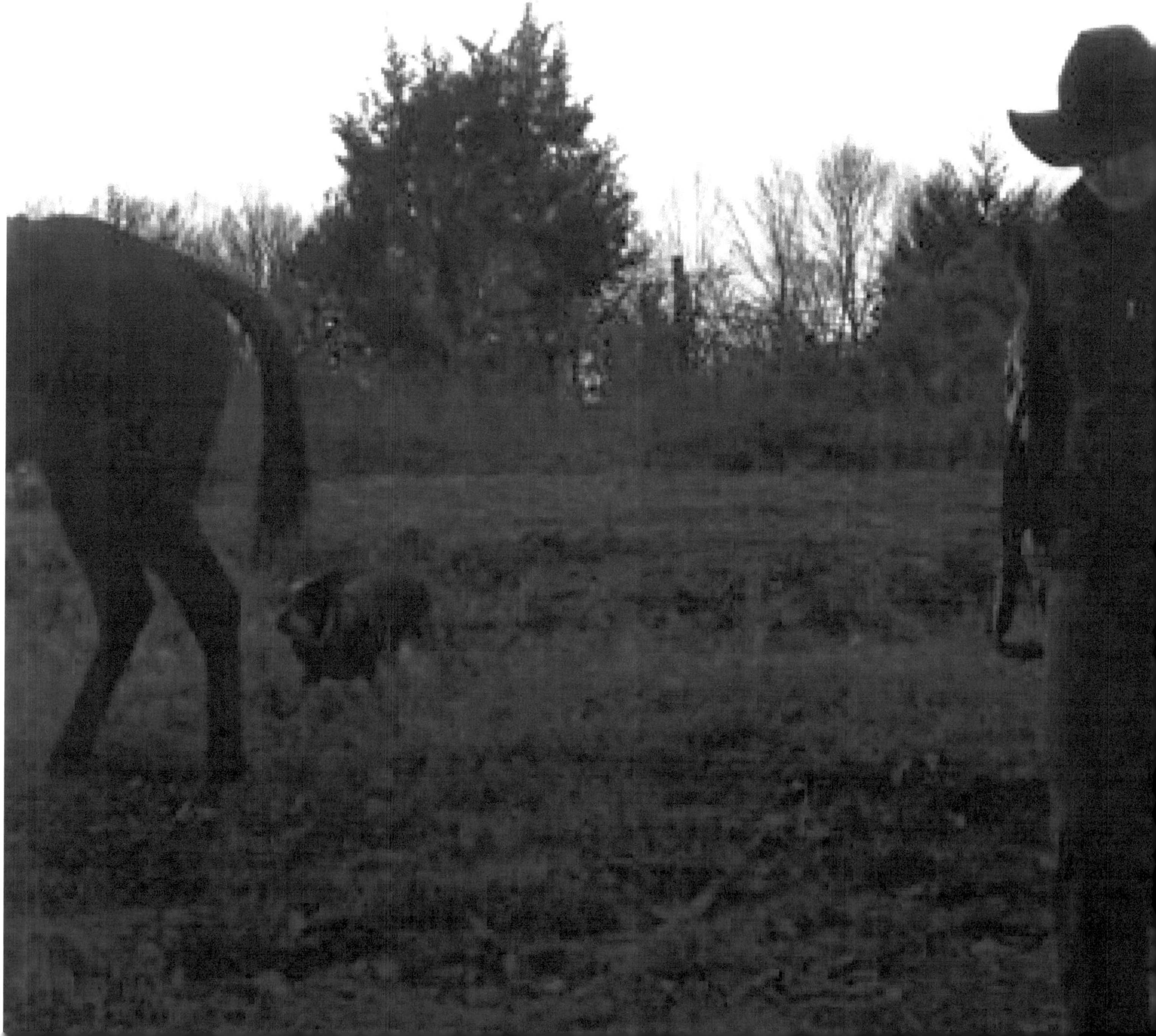

www.ingramcontent.com/pod-product-compliance
Lightning Source LLC
Chambersburg PA
CBHW050906180526
45159CB00007B/2812
* 9 7 8 1 5 0 8 6 1 1 6 1 5 *